CROSS-ENTERPRISE LEADERSHIP

CROSS-ENTERPRISE LEADERSHIP

LEADERSHIP

Business Leadership for the Twenty-First Century

Richard Ivey School of Business
Edited by Dr. Mary Crossan, Dr. Jeffrey Gandz, and Dr. Gerard Seijts
Foreword by Ivey Dean, Carol Stephenson

JOSSEY-BASS
A Wiley Imprint
www.josseybass.com

The article in Chapter 1 was first published in the May/June 2006 *Ivey Business Journal*; an earlier version of the article in Chapter 2 was published in the Jan/Feb 2005 *Ivey Business Journal*; and the article in Chapter 3 was first published in the July/August 2008 *Ivey Business Journal* (www.iveybusinessjournal.com).

Library and Archives Canada Cataloguing in Publication Data

Cross-enterprise leadership : business leadership for the twenty-first century / Richard Ivey School of Business ; edited by Mary Crossan, Jeffrey Gandz, and Gerard Seijts ; foreword by Carol Stephenson.

Includes bibliographical references and index.
ISBN 978-0-470-67940-1

1. Leadership. 2. Success in business. I. Crossan, Mary M II. Gandz, Jeffrey, 1944– III. Seijts, Gerard H IV. Richard Ivey School of Business

HD57.7.C7654 2010   658.4'092   C2010-904383-9

Production Credits
Interior design and layout: Mike Chan
Cover design: Pat Loi
Cover images: ©iStockphoto.com
Printer: Solisco Tri-Graphic

John Wiley & Sons Canada, Ltd.
6045 Freemont Blvd.
Mississauga, Ontario
L5R 4J3

Printed in Canada
1 2 3 4 5 STG 14 13 12 11 10

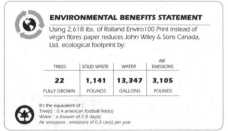

ENVIRONMENTAL BENEFITS STATEMENT
Using 2,618 lbs. of Rolland Enviro100 Print instead of virgin fibres paper reduces John Wiley & Sons Canada, Ltd. ecological footprint by:

TREES	SOLID WASTE	WATER	AIR EMISSIONS
22	1,141	13,347	3,105
FULLY GROWN	POUNDS	GALLONS	POUNDS

It's the equivalent of :
Tree(s) : 0.4 american football field(s)
Water : a shower of 2.8 day(s)
Air emissions : emissions of 0.3 car(s) per year

JB JOSSEY-BASS™

We would like to acknowledge our colleagues, business leaders and students who have been so supportive of this book; Ivey staff Maura Pare, Stephen Bernhut and Penni Pring for their critical roles in enabling the project; and Karen Milner and Lindsay Humphreys, who shepherded the book on behalf of Wiley.

We dedicate this book as follows:

Mary Crossan:
To Larry, Corey and Matthew who provide
unwavering support in everything I do

Jeffrey Gandz:
To Elizabeth

Gerard Seijts:
To my mom and dad who have always been there for me, and
to Jana, Aiden and Arianna for giving me all the happiness

Table of Contents

~Contributors~

William Aziz
Chief Restructuring Officer, Hollinger Inc.
President, BlueTree Advisors Inc.

Tima Bansal, PhD
Professor of Strategy
Director, Building Sustainable Value Research Centre
Executive Director, Network for Business Sustainability
MBA '80 Faculty Fellow

Paul Beamish, PhD
Professor of International Business
Director, Ivey Publishing
Director, Asian Management Institute
Director, Engaging Emerging Markets Research Centre
Donald L. Triggs Chair in International Business
Canada Research Chair in International Management
Fellow of the Royal Society of Canada

Mary Crossan, PhD
Professor of Strategic Management
Taylor Mingay Chair in Business Policy

Jeffrey Gandz, PhD
Professor of General Management
Managing Director, Program Design—Executive
    Development

Jim Hatch, PhD
Professor of Finance

Ashleigh Nimigan
Communications Specialist, Public Affairs

Fernando Olivera, PhD
Associate Professor of Organizational Behaviour

Simon Parker, PhD
Associate Professor of Entrepreneurship
Director, Driving Growth through Entrepreneurship
    and Innovation Research Centre
MBA '80 Professor in Entrepreneurship

Stephen Sapp, PhD
Associate Professor of Finance
Bank of Montreal Faculty Fellow

Gerard Seijts, PhD
Associate Professor of Organizational Behaviour
Director, Leading Cross-Enterprise Research Centre
Ivey Alumni Association/Toronto Faculty Fellow in
    Business Leadership

Carol Stephenson, O.C.
Dean
Lawrence G. Tapp Chair in Leadership

Mark Vandenbosch, PhD
Professor of Marketing
Kraft Professor in Marketing

Michael Wood
General Management Doctoral Candidate

~Foreword~

The Urgent Need for Cross-Enterprise Leadership

BY DEAN CAROL STEPHENSON, RICHARD IVEY SCHOOL OF BUSINESS

In the lingering aftermath of the global economic recession, leadership is in crisis. Questions remain unanswered. How could leaders in the financial services industry—and the regulators who oversee these markets—not anticipate the folly of lending money to people who could not afford a home? Why did leaders in the automobile industry keep manufacturing more and more vehicles in the face of growing overcapacity and declining sales? Moreover, in this age of globalization, how could leaders not foresee that the toxic practices in one part of the world would inevitably poison markets and economies worldwide?

Imagine what might have happened if business and government leaders had better appreciated the interconnectedness of different organizations, markets and economies. Imagine if more leaders had focused on long-term results, not just short-term returns. Imagine if more leaders had acted with vision, honesty and integrity. I have no doubt that the outcome would have been much different—and much better—for economies, for industries, for markets and for the customers, investors and employees who play a role in them.

For all of us at the Richard Ivey School of Business, the ongoing repercussions of the recent economic crisis underscore the urgency for a new leadership approach—an approach that we call cross-enterprise leadership.

Cross-enterprise leaders see the big picture and understand how it is evolving. They are able to anticipate the effect of economic trends, competitive challenges and global-scale market issues. And they know how to capitalize on the synergies that result from gaining this fulsome perspective. That's precisely how cross-enterprise leaders build and sustain the profitability and growth of their enterprises.

Five years ago, our team at the Richard Ivey School of Business set out to examine the impact of globalization, technological innovation and volatile change on leadership. We conducted extensive research, analysis and consultation with our clients and stakeholders across the globe. We uncovered an inherent need across all organizations for cross-enterprise leadership.

Cross-enterprise leaders have a deep understanding of how events, decisions and actions affect the "enterprise"—or the rich complexity of interdependencies both within the organization and between the organization and the environment in which it operates. They look beyond the organizational charts, knowledge silos and walls of their organizations to uncover the full scope of opportunities and challenges facing their organizations.

Cross-enterprise leaders act decisively—and they act quickly. They appreciate that in today's often unpredictable environment, playing it safe or taking it slow just does not make sense. In this era of instant messaging, social networking and ubiquitous wireless communications, real-time competition is the reality. Organizations can no longer afford the luxury of long planning horizons. A predisposition to "wait and see" simply doesn't cut it anymore. Yet, neither does a singular focus on the short term.

Moreover, cross-enterprise leaders know that the old hierarchical command and control approach is grossly ineffective. Instead, these leaders depend on their influence, not on the power of their position. As a result, they develop an acute understanding of the positions of various stakeholders within their enterprise, including their employees. They are capable of identifying potential partners, of initiating and maintaining relationships, of resolving conflicts and of reconfiguring their relationships. Furthermore, they are comfortable dealing with the fluid dynamism inherent in nurturing these relationships. However, they can be decisive and directive when need be. They recognize what approach is needed in the situation.

This book explains how leaders can step up to today's leadership challenges, as it examines the implications of the latest research and experience of organizations operating, or seeking to operate, in emerging markets such as China and India. It looks at driving business growth through entrepreneurship and innovation, leveraging Ivey's work with rapid growth firms. It investigates how organizations and their leaders can create sustainable value in a world where economic issues intertwine with social concerns. In addition, this book dissects cross-enterprise leadership, looking at how organizations and individuals can learn, adapt and enhance their ability to compete effectively.

With globalization, the integration of markets and the rapid advance of communications and information systems, business is brimming with opportunities and endless possibilities. But the challenges are huge. The loci of global trade have shifted dramatically. The people of the world are mixing and mingling more than ever before. Certainly, technology will have more surprises in store. At the same time, the boundaries among companies and industries will continue to blur. And customers will have the power to reward and punish companies as never before.

The business environment today is awash in change—volatile, often unpredictable and always daunting change. In this complex, transformational environment the best leaders know their own stuff cold, but also understand the bigger picture. They can make decisions quickly and effectively, even in times of great uncertainty. And they are compassionate leaders who appreciate the value of integrity, open communications and collaboration in all their relationships.

This book will show you how you can become such a leader, and why you must. The business world needs this caliber of leadership. It needs cross-enterprise leaders—now.

~1~

A New Approach for the 21st Century

BY MARY CROSSAN AND FERNANDO OLIVERA

While the environment of business has become global and more complex, the organization as we know it has remained static and hierarchical. What's needed is a dynamic "enterprise," one that bases leadership and managing on a broad, issues-based platform, not the narrow, turf-protecting expertise of a single department. Enter cross-enterprise leadership.

Cross-enterprise leadership is a holistic approach to value creation in the enterprise. It recognizes four emergent realities that redefine general management for the challenges of the 21st-century manager. First, whereas general management focused on integrating the various functions within an organization, the business imperative today requires an approach—cross-enterprise leadership—that can create, capture and distribute value across a network of companies, not just within a company. Second, these networks, which we call enterprises, are complex and dynamic and must be able to respond as a whole to the emergent challenges that are continually presented. Third, no one leader can "manage" the enterprise, and therefore leadership should be distributed. Finally, these changes require an approach to leadership over and above that possessed by traditional business leaders.

At its core, cross-enterprise leadership recognizes that managers operate in a complex world in which the boundaries of organizations are fluid and dynamic, cutting across functional designations, departments, business units, companies, geography and cultures. Cross-enterprise leadership represents the next generation of general management. This evolution of management education, practice and research requires augmenting the traditional functional focus beyond an integrative emphasis, to build an approach that transcends the functions and the organization. The thrust of this chapter is to describe cross-enterprise leadership. Other chapters to follow will tackle the implications for management education, research and practice.

Cross-Enterprise Leadership Elements

The words "cross-enterprise leadership" pack a lot of meaning. As Table 1 summarizes, and as the sections that follow detail, there are critical differences between general management and cross-enterprise leadership. The word "enterprise" shifts the emphasis from organization, which has a more static orientation and where boundaries are more clearly defined, to enterprise as an action-oriented, value-creating community, where the boundaries of the organization are unclear and

TABLE 1: Differentiating General Management and Cross-Enterprise Leadership

ELEMENT	GENERAL MANAGEMENT	CROSS-ENTERPRISE LEADERSHIP
Entity	Within organizations Boundaries defined	Enterprise—a network of value-adding entities Boundaries unclear
Context	Generally stable and predictable Longer planning horizons	Complex and uncertain Dynamic Real-time
Leadership	Hierarchical Managerial focus	Distributed Management and leadership focus
Orientation	Functional anchor	Issues anchor
Educational approach	Knowledge	Think-act-lead

often in flux. The concept of "cross" emphasizes that there are necessary links across these boundaries and that value creation is not achieved by the components themselves, but in the enterprise's ability to connect the components, thereby informing a dynamic and much more comprehensive approach to leadership than the static, single perspective approach of traditional leadership. "Leadership" in this context shifts from a hierarchical command-and-control approach to a distributed leadership model. The move from general "management" to cross-enterprise "leadership" emphasizes that leadership is the aim. In addition, leaders today need to manage in a context that is far more complex and uncertain, and where time-based competition has become a fact of life. All of these elements have implications for management development in terms of moving beyond functions to issues, and moving beyond imparting knowledge to a more action-oriented approach, which we refer to as "think-act-lead."

From Organization to Enterprise

A central element that distinguishes cross-enterprise leadership from general management is the entity itself. Management education and practice have focused on the organization, where the boundaries of the firm are well defined. Leadership in that context is different from leadership of an enterprise. In an enterprise, there is a network of value-adding entities and the boundaries can be very fuzzy. Alliances, joint ventures and strategic partnerships have enabled the traditional organization to adapt to an increasingly complex world. However, we need to shift our emphasis from the organization to the enterprise to understand what it takes to create and capture value, and lead in this new context.

A striking example of the fuzziness of organizational boundaries is the fact that firms compete in some areas yet cooperate in others. For example, Coca-Cola and Nestlé are competitors in bottled water and several beverage categories around the world. But in North America, Coca-Cola is the primary distributor for Nestlé's Nestea product. In fact, consumers may not even know which organization is actually serving them. For example, UPS undertakes the repairs of Toshiba products—no need to incur the cost or delay in shipping the broken item all the way back to Toshiba. Singapore-based Flextronics undertakes design and manufacturing services for a range of companies in the automotive, industrial, medical and technology sectors. They help customers design, build, ship and service electronic products through their global network spanning 30 countries. As well, there are many logistics providers whose trucks can be customized to represent a particular client, where the employees will even wear the uniform of that client.

"Enterprise" emphasizes the multiple and complex interdependencies that exist in a network of value-creating activities.

From pharmaceuticals to music, the interdependencies and network of value-creating activities are paramount. While some pharmaceutical companies have emphasized developing networks of relationships with other research organizations, others, such as GlaxoSmithKline, have broken up their organization into smaller biotech-style organizations in the hope of creating a more entrepreneurial environment. As Andrew Jack of the *Financial Times* suggests, it "presents challenges to ensure that all the information generated on different sites in self-contained units around the world can be effectively coordinated and shared across a multinational network." This is the essence of cross-enterprise leadership.

Consider the success of the Apple iPod and iTunes. To focus simply on Apple would miss the mark. One needs to look at the broader context, namely the entertainment industry and beyond, to understand Apple's success. First, where others failed to gain buy-in from the recording companies, Steve Jobs was able to craft a solution that bought their support and thereby allowed Apple to escape the vicious assault the Recording Industry Association of America had been waging on Internet music providers. In contrast, though Sony possessed the technology and the music, internal battles prevented the company from pulling these two key pieces together. Where Sony failed, Apple succeeded by partnering with a variety of stakeholders. Like Nestlé, Apple needed to figure out how far to push the boundaries of the enterprise to encompass its own competitors, by making iTunes compatible with Microsoft Windows. Apple's challenges have been predominantly to work with this wide collection of stakeholders, rather than within their own organization. Yet cross-enterprise leadership is not simply about the enterprise itself, but more broadly about the environment in which it operates.

Stability to Dynamic Complexity

Markets are global, and industry and organizational boundaries are often difficult to define. The pace of change is dramatic in many quarters. As a result, the luxury of long planning horizons has diminished as real-time competition becomes a reality. There is more information than we can fathom, yet identifying and managing knowledge is a challenge, placing a huge premium on judgment and responsiveness. Many of our management practices and approaches to leadership were developed for more stable and predictable contexts than exist today. Unfortunately, leaning heavily on old management techniques is no longer effective. Just like musicians who must change their technique to play at a higher tempo, we need to augment our approaches to management to deal with the pace of change. And yet, it is not just the pace of change, but also the uncertainty and associated implications for planning (or lack thereof) that must be addressed. In the case of music, the jazz musician needs to have more capabilities than the orchestral musician in order to improvise. Unfortunately, most managers operate like the traditional orchestra—waiting to do their written part. However, the business environment does not offer the same level of certainty that orchestral music provides. Rather, business is more like jazz, created in real time.

Our research on improvisation suggests that management approaches for dealing with complexity, uncertainty and real-time creation do exist. However, they are, for the most part, not used. One of the first problems is that many managers simply can't "see" it. As the esteemed management guru Karl Weick suggests, people operate as if they will "believe it when they see it," but actually, we tend to "see what we believe." So, we need to start with what we believe in order to see our environment in its full richness and complexity. Removing organization blinders is a first step. Understanding that an enterprise is more than the traditional organization begins to reveal both problems and opportunities that span boundaries. The Apple iPod initiative certainly demonstrates this. Where Apple was able to look beyond its organization and industry to consider the possibilities inherent in music, Sony Corporation, with platforms in both technology and music, was unsuccessful in pulling them together. Apple is now leveraging its expertise in the music industry to develop a range of on-demand communication and entertainment initiatives.

When there is no plan, or music score in the case of jazz, the team is creating in real time. Teams need to learn to deal with complexity and ambiguity. Our research reveals a variety of techniques for doing this. For example, improvisation training helps managers to "see" differently, but it goes further. Nevertheless, improvisation is just one example of how management education and practice needs to consider new approaches to deal with the contexts that have changed.

Leadership for a New Context

Although many would argue that general management incorporates leadership, the emphasis is largely on "management." Of course there have been many debates about the differences, if any, between management and leadership. Whatever the theoretical debating points are, there is a tangible difference in practice. Who cannot describe someone who they think can manage but not lead, and also someone they think can lead but not manage? There is no doubt we need both, but we can't assume that good managers will automatically become good leaders.

Leadership in a context where organizational boundaries are blurry and time-based competition dictates rapid change means that the old hierarchical approach is not sufficient. Distributed leadership approaches are necessary because no one individual can manage it all. Similarly, the "power" of a position becomes less relevant in an enterprise, where different stakeholders come together to influence outcomes. Many would suggest that it was Jobs' ability to influence the record companies that enabled Apple to successfully secure the inventory of music for iTunes.

Shifting the focus from power to influence emphasizes a range of issues, from understanding the various stakeholder positions to being able to work collaboratively within the network. Leaders must be capable of identifying potential partners, initiating and maintaining relationships, resolving conflicts and reconfiguring their relationships. Furthermore, cross-enterprise leadership means that leaders will be comfortable dealing with ambiguity, uncertainty, complexity and time pressures while leveraging these relationships.

Distributed leadership means that leading cross-enterprise is not only necessary for those at the top of the organization, but that it is even more essential at lower levels of the organization, where there isn't a natural cross-enterprise vantage point. Those at the top tend to see more of the organization and the industry landscape—they see the forest rather than the trees. Those at lower levels see the trees and are more challenged to see the forest. However, it is this very capability that is essential for distributed leadership, as these individuals are likely to be the nexus within the network and the point of contact with external stakeholders.

Cross-enterprise leadership is relevant for every business, whether it be large or small, domestic or multinational. Consider the extremes. Small, domestic entrepreneurial companies are, by their very nature, cross-enterprise because the founders rarely have a full set of resources to implement the plan. Much of the context they face is uncertain and ambiguous, and entrepreneurs will tell you that they need to adjust on the fly. Equally, the large multinational company is inherently complex and cross-enterprise means crossing functions, levels, business lines, geographies and companies.

From Functions to Issues

Management education and management practice have been anchored in functions, or what academics refer to as disciplines. The last two decades have seen phenomenal growth in the body of knowledge and associated expertise in the field of management. Drawing on disciplines such as economics, psychology and sociology, business schools developed their own acumen in areas such as finance and marketing. Faculty became experts in these areas and spawned many generations of business graduates with strong functional expertise. A general management orientation traditionally was achieved by integrative courses that drew on all functional areas. The flaws of this approach have been apparent for some time. In fact, the "silo mentality" of business is a direct result of this functional focus. In business schools, the proliferation of new courses in areas such as entrepreneurship, international management and information management suggests that the traditional functional orientation does not cover the territory. And clearly, the changing environment of business exposes the vulnerability of current business models.

Consider an issue on the minds of most business leaders: innovation. Growth through innovation is one of the primary means to drive shareholder value. However, innovation has not been dealt with very well by the functional disciplines in business schools. Even when the topic is covered, it is done so in piecemeal fashion, with little or no integration across the disciplines. Although lack of integration is a problem, the bigger problem is that innovation is not inherently a functional type of issue! Understanding innovation requires us to draw on an incredibly diverse knowledge base. Aspects of that knowledge base are strewn throughout academic research and management practice, and rarely drawn together in a holistic sense in the classroom or beyond. Consider where the mandate for innovation lies within a business. At first blush it is difficult to pin down, and a quick second glance suggests that it is everywhere. Yet few business leaders know how to tackle it. Innovation is indeed complex. It not only requires working with the resources of the business, but also collaborating cross-enterprise with many other organizations, often in a global context. In his bestselling book *The World Is Flat,* Thomas Friedman describes how business innovation spans organizations and the globe. Take, for example, the California accounting firm that outsources tax returns to a company in India that completes them at lower cost, faster turnaround (given the time difference), and with similar, if not better, quality.

When we begin to examine business issues from a cross-enterprise fashion we are in a better position to understand the problems and opportunities. Narrow functional or cross-functional perspectives drastically limit the possibilities. From a management education standpoint this is somewhat of a "back to the future" orientation. Before the tremendous bodies of functional knowledge emerged, the focus was on issues. The challenge today is to build on the functional knowledge without being a prisoner of it. As the foregoing suggests, there is much more to cross-enterprise leadership than integrating functional competencies.

From Knowledge to Think-Act-Lead

If you walk into an MBA class in many business schools, you likely will sit through a lecture in Finance, Marketing or Accounting. But thinking cross-enterprise goes beyond understanding theories and how they can be integrated. It requires understanding the complexity of business issues from all angles, not just from a functional perspective. That understanding spans functions, levels of the organization, business units, companies, geographies and cultures.

Acting in a cross-enterprise fashion extends understanding of complex issues to develop the capacity to make decisions and implement them in an environment filled with uncertainty and complexity. Textbook learning of theories does little to develop an action orientation. Being action oriented when faced with uncertainty, complexity and time pressure "ups the ante." Borrowing from the experiences of hospital emergency rooms, firefighting and crisis management, where time is a scarce resource, we know that making decisions and taking actions in these contexts is different than when we have plenty of time to think and act, and when options are clearly defined. How quickly can credit card companies respond to the threat by Japanese mobile phone operator NTT, who is launching a credit card service over its mobile phones? Some may end up partnering while others may end up competing. Whatever the course of action, time is at a premium in being able to respond. Cross-enterprise leaders have the capacity to act in contexts that are much more dynamic than they once were.

Finally, leading cross-enterprise is not for the faint of heart. It means that individuals have the capacity to deal with ambiguity and complexity, and more importantly, rally others to do so as well. Cross-enterprise means that these "others" may reside in other parts of the organization, other organizations, or other geographies or cultures, and in most cases the leader may be operating without power and authority and must rely almost entirely on influence. It would be a mistake to characterize these leaders in a heroic fashion, as is the case in so many business schools and businesses. On the contrary, operating with influence, under ambiguous and complex circumstances and across the many divides, requires the development of leadership characteristics that often have been at odds with traditional business education and management practice. Cross-enterprise leaders are confident about what they do, but they also have a healthy dose of humility since they are always in a learning mode. They are aggressive about achieving results but also smart enough to recognize that patience is important. They are analytical but also rely on intuition. We can select for these kinds of characteristics, but it is also our responsibility to develop and promote what it takes to lead cross-enterprise.

Although cross-enterprise leadership is a new term, it essentially redefines general management for the challenges of today. The redefinition is, however, not trivial. How we choose to define ourselves drives our priorities in both management education and practice. Cross-enterprise leadership demands a shift from focusing on the organization to the enterprise, and a shift from being anchored in functions to being anchored in business issues, which by their nature are cross-enterprise. Just as we need to build on the strengths of the functions, and of general management, we need to radically rethink how we will employ those strengths in the service of cross-enterprise leadership.

~2~

What Cross-Enterprise Leaders DO!

BY JEFFREY GANDZ

Leadership is about getting results for your followers. If you get results, people will support you; without results, all the style or charisma in the world won't retain the support of your followers for long. This is true for the leader of a Scout troop, a sports team, a political party, a government department . . . and a business. Business leaders must increase shareholder value by growing earnings per share and reducing the volatility of those earnings in the short term. Whatever else they do, without this short-term achievement business leaders have no long-term future, especially if they are running public companies with impatient shareholders.

But we look to business leaders to do more than this. The best of them, the *cross-enterprise leaders*, will perform for the short run, *and* ensure the sustainability of their organizations over the longer term, *and* do their analysis and make their decisions in ways that benefit the whole enterprise, not just the part of it with which they are affiliated or the function they perform. To do this they

- understand, appreciate and interpret the environment in which they operate
- develop winning strategies focused on clearly defined goals
- execute them brilliantly, aligning all elements of the organization in support of their strategies
- measure the quality of the execution and the impact of the strategies systematically and in real-time, adjusting strategies as indicated
- build the capabilities, capacity and the culture for sustainable future growth
- optimize performance and development of the total enterprise

The Leadership Role

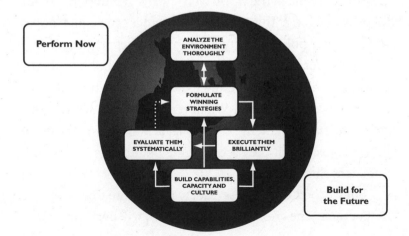

Analyze the Environment in Which
the Enterprise Operates

A leader has to be able to sense what's coming up ahead, to see opportunities that should be the target of action and to identify threats before they materialize. The view has to extend well into the future. As a colleague of mine once noted, "It's no good mistaking the edge of the rut for the horizon."[1]

Leaders who can only see what they have seen before, whose scope and vision is limited by their past experience, prove to be inadequate in a rapidly changing world. We expect leaders to have their feet on the ground, their eyes on the horizon, and their imaginations beyond it.

Looking over the horizon does not suggest that experience is irrelevant. On the contrary, to the extent that people have been through experiences and learned from them, they will usually have developed judgment and, perhaps, some wisdom. Effective leaders do learn from the mistakes of history so that they can avoid repeating them. But the future seldom offers up exactly the same set of conditions that existed yesterday, and tomorrow's environment must be interpreted in the light of yesterday's experience—but seldom with exactly the same mental map or template. Experience that results in a rigid way of thinking about the world may be detrimental when the world changes. We saw this in the collapse of the financial markets in 2008 when it was clear that the implicit or explicit business models used both by financial institutions and regulators did not consider that a drop in house prices was even possible. These models had been built by people whose experiences had been only of rising house prices.

---

1 Professor Richard [Dick] Hodgson, a gifted teacher of Leadership at the Western Business School, often used this phrase.

Business opportunities often are created or destroyed by both direct influences of economic, political, societal and technological forces as well as complex interactions between these forces. Whole industries were created by the development of the transistor; socialized medicine limits the growth of medical services in many countries; periods of economic growth and slowdown, or realignment of currencies, affect businesses in many ways; and political movements to the right or the left may create opportunities for the private sector to grow or, sometimes, may result in the state taking over functions from private enterprise. Those who foresaw the fall of the Berlin Wall, the emergence of China and India as two of the world's great economies, the resistance of many countries to genetically modified foodstuffs, the dramatic realignment of the U.S. dollar against the euro and other currencies in the early part of this century, the eventual bursting of the property bubble that led to the financial meltdown of 2008–2009 made fortunes. Those who did not read their environments correctly lost them.

This outward- and forward-looking requirement cannot be delegated to a small set of specialized scenario-creators or confined to a few days or weeks of the year. The chief financial officer must scan the financial environment, the head of human resources must be alert to changes in labor markets and legislation that affects the workforce, and the chief information officer must recognize developments in information technology that could create or destroy competitive advantage.

Nor is looking at the developing environment required solely of senior executives; the credit manager must look at rising consumer debt levels, the purchasing manager must think of commodity price movements and the things that influence them, the facilities manager must decide whether to go long or short on energy prices...and so on. Leadership at *all* levels must be focused on the future as well as the present.

Formulate Winning Strategies

If leadership is about getting results, then the role of the leader is to develop the right strategies to get those results—*winning* strategies.

Strategies are much more than intentions; they describe what an organization is going to do to achieve a defined end as well as the ways and means that will be employed to do that. The what and the how are usually accompanied by strategic plans detailing who will do what, with which resources, by when... and all the other details that allow for effective and efficient capital and people allocation and coordination. Since people generally follow leaders better when they understand why they are being asked to move in a certain direction, strategies usually provide cogent reasons for action.

Strategies are needed at all levels of organizations, from the office of the CEO to the individual salesperson's strategy for their territory. And these strategies must be integrated and coordinated if they are to be well executed. My emphasis is on developing *winning* strategies, where "winning" is defined as meeting goals. People who lead their followers in the wrong directions may be effective leaders over the short run. And the short run may be quite a long run! But if the pathway chosen leads to eventual disaster, there will be no place for such leaders in the leadership hall of fame.

Execute Those Strategies—Brilliantly!

Strategies are only valuable if they can be executed well. And execution of any plan is only valuable if the strategy is right. Arguing which is more important, therefore, is pointless. Both are critical to success.

Unique strategies are rare. Some years ago I received a copy of the marketing strategies and plans of a large bank before I had signed a confidentiality agreement. A day later, I received a phone call from a very agitated executive asking me to return them immediately. I did so, but without adding that they were indistinguishable from the strategies of four other banks that I had reviewed in the previous three years. The competitive advantage is unlikely to come from the uniqueness of the strategies; far more likely, the company that executes the strategy with brilliance will win.

There are many elements that go into the execution of strategies. Key among them are the following:

- the alignment of the organization's various department and sub-unit strategies so each and every unit and person is striving to achieve goals and objectives that contribute to the overall mission, vision and objectives
- performance management, at the individual, team, departmental and organizational unit levels, to ensure that the right people are recruited, trained, developed, motivated and directed in ways that support the organization's mission, vision and objectives consistent with organizational values
- the leadership of strategic and operational change, not just in response to "burning platforms" but in anticipation of events and states that many people in the organization cannot comprehend or visualize at the moment when change must be planned and initiated

Many excellent strategic thinkers and planners fall short when it comes to execution. They may lack the attention span needed to concentrate on the details of large-scale organizational change; they may not be persistent enough to see those changes through to completion when faced with resistance to change; they may feel that to do these things is "micromanaging" and that their role is to focus on the "big picture." That is not my view—they must do both! Truly effective leaders *derive* strategy in part from a detailed understanding of their business and how it works, and they *drive* strategy through each and every business decision and the people who make things happen in the organization. They are as tenacious in implementation as they are brilliant in strategic formulation.

Monitor the Results and Make Strategic Adjustments

The perfect strategy, flawlessly executed, is the exception rather than the rule. Leaders recognize the probable imperfections of any plan and take care to monitor the outcomes systematically and thoroughly, always being prepared to make adjustments or completely change the strategy.

The best strategies and plans incorporate measurements, but smart leaders are always alert to the unanticipated: the competitor who responds differently than anticipated; the sales force that cannot recruit enough people of sufficient quality to execute the sales plan, at least on the preconceived schedule; the key research scientist who leaves to join a competitor; an unanticipated change in legislation that makes it impractical or illegal to take a certain approach to the marketplace; a planned merger that ran into trouble in the integration phase; a market that turned sour; a product that did not live up to expectation.

Really effective leaders understand the frailty of strategic plans. Strategic plans are often based on assumptions made months or years before the plans are implemented. They also understand that if they act promptly they often can make mid-course corrections to plans that can put them back on track, or they may even find a superior solution. There is a saying: "If you're going to eat crow, eat it while it's young and tender." Recognizing mistakes quickly and fixing them as quickly is the key to strategic agility. So what if it's a little embarrassing. In its early days, Dell experimented with retail outlets—briefly! Then Michael Dell realized that he was moving away from the direct sales channel that was the core competence of his company. He rapidly changed directions. After a decade of extraordinary success with the direct distribution approach he realized that competitors had caught up with his low cost model through rationalizing their own supply lines so that they could match his low prices. He then started up the retail channels because he needed the additional distribution and also because demand had shifted to notebook computers that potential customers need to see, touch and feel rather than order over the Internet. Unfortunately for Dell and its shareholders, the second switch to retail distribution was probably delayed a couple of years because of the huge success that the company had experienced with direct sales—it was hard to accept that its model was "broken" or, at least, under severe stress.

Highly effective leaders also *increase* their sensitivity to discordant information when they are deploying new strategies. Sam Steinberg, the founder of Miracle Food Mart, had a great saying: "When three people tell you that you're drunk ... lie down!" But that only works if you are listening to the people. Every great historical leader recognized that courtiers were not necessarily the best advisers of kings and queens ... there was the need for the presence of the "voice of the people." So, smart strategic leaders have monitoring systems that feed back what customers, first-line employees, suppliers, regulators and other stakeholders and their representatives are thinking about strategic decisions and their implementation. They don't retreat to their management bunkers and wait for the first official measures of success to be released. They get out there, personally, meet with early adopters, meet with people who have tried the product and did not repurchase, attend testing panels, see how trade channels respond to presentations and so on.

A story is told of Jack Welch, former CEO of General Electric, arriving in a city one day to be met by a local senior general manager. As they were climbing into the car, Welch asked, "Where are we going?" and was told, "To see some of our best customers who would like to meet you." Welch responded, "Cancel it; I want to go see the people who aren't buying from us!" Leaders aren't looking for flattery—they are looking for information that will inform and improve their strategic decisions. Does this personal involvement create some concerns among subordinates that they are not being trusted to do what they are supposed to do? Yes, sometimes. But real leaders don't get too upset about this. They would much rather risk this than have anyone believe that they did *not* sweat the details, and most of those who are responsible for the details are delighted with the leadership attention they are getting.

Build Organizational Capabilities, Capacity and Culture

Highly effective leaders act for both the short *and* the long terms, simultaneously. So, while they are surveying their environments, developing winning strategies and executing them brilliantly, and monitoring them systematically, they are also investing time, effort and money in building their organization's core capabilities, capacity and the kind of culture they will need in the future.

In the real world, managers must often cut costs to meet profit crunches, frequently at the expense of anything that promises long-term returns. Many commodity-focused companies, such as those in basic steel production, respond to downturns in the price of steel or increases in input costs by laying off people in inverse order of seniority, enacting hiring freezes, stopping all recruitment of new people, and postponing or canceling training and leadership development. It's little wonder that after 50 years of doing this, they have aging workforces and reputations as places where you go to stagnate in a role forever rather than to be developed to the maximum of your potential.

The business leader also has a keen eye on costs and, certainly in commodity businesses, is sensitive to the price fluctuations in the marketplace. But unlike the manager, he or she balances the need to cut costs with the mandate to build for the longer term. Employment costs may be cut not by hiring freezes but by buying out two "C" employees and replacing them with an "A," by cutting some lower value training programs but retaining core leadership development programs, and by developing high-potential focused programs. The leader who does this with a cross-enterprise perspective looks for those cuts that would damage the enterprise least, even if that meant cutting deeper in areas closer to home.

Note that we are talking here about leading for the short term *and* the long term. Managers choose between the two, maximizing one or the other; leaders optimize both.

But there is more than leadership strength that must be developed. Other core competencies, such as knowledge management skills, intellectual property, excellence in business–government relations, community acceptability and environmental reputation, all represent valuable assets that can be turned into income or other outcome measures at some time in the future. Leaders add to this store of assets rather than deplete them. Leaders that liquidate core competencies for short-term operating results may not be doing the leadership job that they appear to be doing on the surface. Liquidating an asset may have a temporary positive impact on income, but it also may have a negative effect on the balance sheet when assets are viewed as financial capital, human capital and organizational capital!

Outstanding leaders over the long haul recognize that they must continue to invest in core competencies at the same time that they produce results in the short run. Whether it is renewing a physical plant, equipment, machinery or the talent pool, it represents the future of the organization.

The Challenges of Leadership

I have described three primary challenges of leadership—strategic (involving both environmental surveillance and the formulation of winning strategies), executional (implementing those strategies, monitoring their impact and making adjustments as indicated) and developmental (building capabilities, capacity and culture).

There is another, more personal challenge. Leadership can be frustrating, exciting, exhilarating, depressing, stimulating, dangerous, exhausting and many other things. Throughout, the leader must keep a sense of personal balance, humility and integrity. Leaders must keep growing, learning and developing if they are to continue to be effective leaders. The leader often has responsibilities and obligations beyond the narrow business sphere—to family, community and the broader society within which he or she operates. These must be balanced with the obligations the leader has toward the enterprise he or she leads and the people who put their trust in that leadership.

Leadership is not for everyone, and it is not something that even really good leaders necessarily want to do forever. Above all else, leaders need to know when it is time to stop leading, to hand over the reins to someone else. The leader that outstays his or her willingness or capacity to lead is one who will eventually do poor service to followers, no matter how well he or she may have served them in the past.

~3~

The Cross-Enterprise Leader

BY MARY CROSSAN, JEFFREY GANDZ AND GERARD SEIJTS

The cross-enterprise leader is someone who, at any level of leadership, sees the issues and analyzes them, and then acts with the interests and perspectives of the total enterprise in mind, including any networks or alliances of other enterprises in which it helps create and deliver stakeholder value. He or she avoids narrow business unit, functional or geographical interests in favor of doing the right thing for the enterprise, even if compensation or other reward systems suggest something different.

What's the "secret sauce" that these cross-enterprise leaders have, and what can organizations do to develop them? We have pooled our scholarship in leadership, strategy and organizational effectiveness, and our experience as consultants and executive educators in and with organizations to propose a recipe for this sauce.

The Five Types of Intelligence for Cross-Enterprise Leadership

At a minimum, the cross-enterprise leader needs four types of specific intelligence: business, strategic, organizational and people. By "intelligence" we mean knowledge, understanding of key concepts and relationships between variables, and skills in these four critical areas of executive competence.[1] These must be underpinned by a reasonably high general intellect, the fifth type of intelligence.

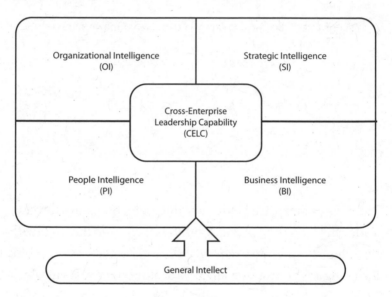

Business Intelligence

There is no shortcut to business intelligence (BI). Leadership is not developed in the abstract and leaders need to understand the

---

1 The terms "executive" and "intelligence" have appeared in prior literature, notably in the work of Justin Menkes in *Executive Intelligence: What All Great Leaders Have*. Executive Intelligence Group (New York: HarperCollins, 2005). However, our use of the terms extend his more restricted view of the competencies, knowledge, values and judgment required by leaders, especially those with cross-enterprise leadership capabilities.

nuts and bolts of the business they are in, whether it be a food bank or a commercial bank. Understanding the economics of the business model, how value is created, how the functions of the business relate to each other, competitive dynamics, customer needs and where the leverage points for improvement reside are essential leadership elements. There is much to know and every business has its nuances. Nick Leeson, the rogue trader whose actions took down Barings Bank, has suggested that leaders in his organization lacked the business competence to question his actions.

Lou Gerstner, the former CEO of IBM who is largely credited with turning around the company, is an example of a leader with high BI. Gerstner came from RJR Nabisco; he did not express an interest in the job of CEO at IBM. He felt that, as a non-technical person, he was not qualified to be at the helm of IBM. But within a short time he learned all he could about the organization and the environment in which it operated. He was a visible leader. A favorite expression of his was, "A desk is a dangerous place from which to view the world."[2]

Many leaders tend to learn the ropes as they go. Thus, it is not surprising that MBA programs and leadership development efforts have served to fill this gap while leaders seek the knowledge they lack. Job rotations have become common in firms like GE and Nokia, to ensure that leaders experience the various facets of business, whether they are human resource management, finance or operations.

The pitfalls we have observed are several:

- Leaders don't know what they don't know. Many underestimate the BI they need. We see many leaders who struggle

2 Louis V. Gerstner Jr., *Who Says Elephants Can't Dance?: Inside IBM's Historic Turnaround* (New York: HarperCollins, 2004).

with financial analysis or have difficulty understanding the drivers of operational excellence, or who may not fully grasp the levers that affect brand management, for example.

- Leaders who are successful in a specialized area are often unwilling to stretch their comfort zone and learn about other facets of the business.
- For those who develop strong BI, the challenge is in knowing these microelements of the business without micromanaging. Leaders with high BI ensure that those who work for and with them develop BI as well.
- Going up the hierarchy of BI, the more you know, the more challenging it is to prioritize—you see everything! Some call this "analysis paralysis." Being able to prioritize comes from seeing those links across the functional areas of the business that create leverage.
- Leaders who have strong BI can often become very insular in their own business, with little concern for others. However, you need to mind your own business while supporting other businesses.
- Having high BI is not enough, because leaders need to understand the links to the three other types of intelligence as well.

Strategic Intelligence

Leaders must have the BI to work *in* the business, but they need the strategic intelligence (SI) to work *on* the business. Part of working on the business requires understanding the strategic context in which it is positioned. This tends to go beyond a simple understanding of customers and competitors to more fundamental elements that drive short- and long-term business success. A leader has to be able to sense what's coming, to see opportunities that should be the target of action and to see threats before they materialize. And the view has to look at a horizon well into the future.

In 2006, the Stratford Festival of Canada celebrated an important milestone—the performance of *Harlem Duet*. The show was the first black work to be produced in the Festival's 54-year history; it had an all-black cast. A critical consideration for putting the show on the playbill was the significant change in demographics over the years and those that would occur in the near future. Executive Director Antoni Cimolino felt that it was important for the future of the Festival that the organization commit to broaden the scope of the stories the Festival told. In his view, it was essential that the Festival take steps to better reflect the diversity of the people from which it drew.

As mentioned in the previous chapter, Richard Hodgson, a colleague of ours at Ivey, used to say, "It's no good mistaking the edge of the rut for the horizon." BI can often be focused on the rut, but SI must be focused on the horizon. So what's challenging about SI?

- Accepted industry practices may not be based on a sound strategic foundation. Bucking industry norms requires thinking about the business from first principles in order to assess whether fundamental assumptions are valid.
- The uncertainties around SI are significant, such as the severity of a downturn or the nature and timing of a competitive response. As well, leaders often fail to fully assess the risk/return trade-off.
- SI is rarely about designing one strategy but rather a set of strategic options that create flexibility and resilience.

- It's difficult to see beyond the share price conundrum. Often, the interests of investors are not aligned with the interest of the company. A company needs to excel in the short term while managing for the long term, meaning that it may have to sacrifice short-term cash flow to generate long-term profits. Why should investors wait for the return when they can buy other undervalued stocks, hold them while they appreciate and then buy back into the stock at a more favorable time?

- Great SI can lead to short-term payoffs but leaders need to be mindful of the longer-term implications. As a tax professor once declared, "Pigs get fat and hogs get slaughtered." Evidence abounds of stakeholders who don't take kindly to the hog. Recording companies are being slaughtered by consumers who feel vindicated in being able to rip them off with "free" music. Many companies have felt the sting of regulators who can quickly turn the tables on a company/industry that has been "greedy." And communities have turned on companies like Wal-Mart when they perceive a serious threat. Harlequin, having monopolized the industry for romance novels for years, found its market share cut in half when Simon & Schuster, offended by having their distribution agreement rescinded, invested millions to attract Harlequin's authors and editors in its bid to buy market share.

- Strong BI can drive out SI, because the expertise and knowledge of the business may create an analytical base that devalues intuition and creativity. As Einstein once said, "The intuitive mind is a sacred gift and the rational mind is a faithful servant. We have created a society that honors the servant and has forgotten the gift."

- Conversely, great SI comes from strong BI, and both can only be realized with strong organizational intelligence (OI) and people intelligence (PI).

Organizational Intelligence

Even those leaders that have PI may not have OI. It is easy for leaders to miss this because the elements of OI tend to be less visible. Jack Welch used to refer to the "social architecture" that forms the foundation for action. Consider the structure, procedures, and compensation systems that tend to hardwire what individuals pay attention to and how they do their work. OI is fundamental and ultimately drives the culture of the organization. Leaders with strong OI understand how organizations work and how to work organizations. They know how and when to use power, influence and persuasion. They understand the dynamics of complex change and how to lead it. The former CEO of Coca-Cola, Douglas Ivester, is an example of a leader who did not measure up against this dimension. Evaluating his leadership, *Business Week* wrote: "The ex-accountant knew the numbers of the soda business cold, but he had a tin ear when it came to the intangibles of being a chief executive, particularly the ability to manage and nurture a cherished brand in a global market."[3]

The pitfalls in acquiring and deploying OI are several:

- As a strong leader, it is easy to underestimate the power and influence of the organization. After all, don't strong leaders excel in spite of the organization? There is plenty of research to show that strong leaders wilt in poorly designed organizations.

---

3 Dean Foust, *Why Coke Didn't Go Better with Ivester*, Business Week Online Briefing, December 6, 1999, http://www.businessweek.com/bwdaily/dnflash/dec1999/nf91206h.htm.

- Since much of an organization is like the iceberg under the water, it is tough to see what to work on and how the pieces of organizational design relate.
- An organization is indeed a type of social architecture. Like a ball of yarn where everything comes unraveled simply by pulling on one string, leaders need to be mindful of how the pieces connect when making changes.
- Having OI is essential, but building the organization that one envisions takes time. It took Welch two decades to build his social architecture. This was in addition to the two previous decades that had brought GE to the strong organization it was when Welch assumed leadership.

People Intelligence

Most of what is written about leadership is about people intelligence (PI). The charismatic, transformational leader is one who understands people and is able to motivate them to achieve extraordinary results. Twists are put on this relationship. One example is the servant leader, who actually serves followers rather than leads them. However, any twist relates to the same point, which is the need to understand individuals and teams and what it takes to support and enable them to have the motivation, capability and direction to contribute. The great leader described by Jim Collins is one who, through "level-5" leadership, embraces the fierce determination and humility that lead to involvement and commitment by his or her followers. These leaders develop a sense of self-efficacy, of value, of worth in their followers who want to be led by such leaders, not because they are sheep but because they understand that they can achieve their goals through those leaders. And they are prepared to exercise leadership themselves within the umbrella of the organizational leader who makes them feel good about themselves.

William Aziz, a turnaround leader, uses the following example to illustrate that leadership is about how you "get along with people."

> I used to go to the docks at two in the morning at Interlink Freight Systems. I was the first president that they had seen in the dock in the middle of the night, and the reason I went there was to see what goes on. I went one time on a truck trip from Toronto to Kingston, switched trucks in Kingston and drove to Montreal. I learned what the truck drivers were talking about, their worries, and found out that if you're a truck driver and you sit in a truck eight hours a day, with a rattle beside your head in the truck, you come out of that truck furious. I came out of that truck in Montreal and I went down to the basement where they had a place where these guys eat breakfast and I sat down by myself, ordered some bacon and eggs. Suddenly one guy came over and he wanted to know who I was. Pretty soon I had about a 100 guys around me, all truck drivers and dock workers who wanted to talk. They'd never seen a president of this company in their little cafeteria.

Without PI, leaders are either ineffective, or their effectiveness is limited to a narrow range of situations:

- The criticism of many consultants is that while they have strong BI or SI, they haven't had to develop enough PI to fully appreciate what it takes to effect change. Not having PI means that BI and SI often contain faulty assumptions. Even if OI is high, actually "making it happen" requires the kind of PI that may be lacking in many leaders.

- The notorious "turnaround" leaders, who have great SI and BI, and even have the OI to understand what needs to be done for the organization to survive, often fail once the immediate crisis passes. They lack the PI to run the surviving, often transformed, entity.

Yet it should be clear from the discussions above that PI alone does not make for a good leader, never mind a great leader. The effective leader of people who has the wrong strategy—formulated because SI and BI were lacking—merely hastens the demise of the organization. And one who can lead people as individuals or in teams, but who lacks the OI to move the larger enterprise, will be equally as ineffective.

General Intellect

Being smart matters! Intellect plays a key role in leadership. It allows people to analyze cause-and-effect relationships, to understand multivariate models with complex interactions and to isolate the effects of independent variables such as currency fluctuations, commodity prices, competitive actions, changing consumer demands and a host of others on some important, dependent variable, such as ROI. Strong intellect gives leaders confidence that they can understand complex issues and can encourage them to use their intuition.

Often, and perhaps surprisingly, the need for a high level of general intellect is either overlooked or wrongly assumed to be in place. Some suggest that the recent global liquidity crisis can be traced to a number of players who clearly did not understand what they were getting into or the risks they were taking. No doubt many articles and books will be written about this in the years to come, but our bet is that a simple lack of basic smarts will emerge as a significant variable underlying at least some of the behaviors of some key people in this situation.

While necessary, being intellectually smart is not a *sufficient* condition for cross-enterprise leadership; intellect can easily drive out the development of the other dimensions. We have encountered too many leaders and people in leadership positions who think it is all about how bright they are. Their very brightness is then used as an excuse or apology for not developing the BI, SI, OI and PI that they need to be effective cross-enterprise leaders.

Of our five "intelligences," four (BI, SI, OI and PI) can be learned, while general intellect is something that you are born with ... or not. Nevertheless, it is undoubtedly true that people of lesser intellect can become very good leaders by working hard at the other things that do not come naturally. Again, our own experience with MBA students indicates that those who score in the top 60–70 percent of the graduate management admissions test can develop the BI, SI, OI and PI required for a leader to be effective. Still, the higher the levels of intellect that one brings to the game, the better the likely outcome.

Cross-Enterprise Leadership Capability

We have described the five basic ingredients of cross-enterprise leadership capability (CELC); however, it is the recipe itself that is the real secret sauce—the ability to synthesize, integrate and sequence the levers of BI, SI, OI, PI and the underlying GI. It is this ability that lies at the heart of cross-enterprise leadership.

Although many books have been written about BI, SI, OI and PI, few highlight the importance of having all of them. This is not surprising, since each has evolved from different disciplines. For example, the psychological base of PI is quite different from the economic and political base of SI. OI finds its roots in sociology and anthropology. And BI tends to arise from specialized knowledge in areas such as operations, finance, marketing and IT. The point is that it takes enormous breadth to understand each of these areas. Therefore it is not surprising that they are compartmentalized when it comes to articles, books and even many leadership development programs.

But make no mistake about this: Considering or having just one type of intelligence without the others is not only suboptimal, it can be dangerous. For example, having great PI without SI and BI generally means that people are engaged, but about the wrong things! SI without OI is what we tend to call good industry analysis without any understanding of how the organization will execute it. Many strategies fail because of poor execution, because leaders don't understand the organizational capabilities and resources required to execute the strategy. There are many leaders with strong BI that can't seem to grasp SI, and there are individuals with strong SI and weak BI. Neither type of leader will perform well, since they need to see both the forest and the trees to be effective.

Understanding the connection among BI, SI, OI and PI means more than being competent in each area. Having the capacity to anticipate the dynamics of the interrelationships is critical to ensuring that leaders are able to sequence actions in a way that leverages or strengthens a particular area. Every leader and every organization will have strengths and weaknesses in each area. The leadership challenge is to diagnose those strengths and weaknesses to consider the best sequence of actions.

The synthesis and sequencing of BI, SI, OI and PI are core dimensions of CELC, but there are other aspects as well. In fact, we see the core of CELC as a set of leadership attributes that provide the engine for development of all of the areas. It has been said that the only sustainable competitive advantage for organizations is their capacity to learn. The same can be said for leaders. Below, we outline a set of attributes that are grounded in a learning orientation of the cross-enterprise leader. Much can be said about these essential qualities. We draw on the extensive work of Christopher Peterson and Martin Seligman, who have amassed an 800-page compendium of research that helps to identify the character strengths and virtues that have global appeal.[4] They identify six virtues along with their associated character strengths. When we put their list together with our experiences it creates a definition of the character elements essential to effective cross-enterprise leadership:

- **Wisdom.** Creativity, curiosity, open-mindedness, love of learning and perspective are critical to deepening and developing one's leadership capability. A key aspect of this learning capability is dealing with complexity and ambiguity. As one executive described it, "It is okay to get caught in the headlights but it is not okay to be frozen in them."

- **Temperateness.** Being temperate involves curbing the tendency to excess, which entails having modesty, self-control and humility. The leader who thinks he or she knows everything is not in a very good position to learn. Furthermore, learning often arises from making mistakes and many

---

4 *Character Strengths and Virtues* (New York: Oxford University Press, 2004).

leaders do not want to admit mistakes to themselves or others. Many leaders fall short in this area because they assume that being a leader means they have all the answers.

- **Integrity.** Having an ethical worldview that you can articulate and rely on to wade through messy and challenging leadership issues is essential. We have encountered many leaders who have no moral compass and who tend to lose their way as a result. Peterson and Seligman referred to this as a sense of "justice." It is the preparedness as a leader "to do the right thing in the right way" all of the time and to be a coherent, authentic person both in one's persona as a formal organizational leader and as a private individual. The leader with integrity does not abandon that when he or she walks into the office, no matter how tempting it can be to take the most expedient approach when that road leads away from the ethical path.

- **Compassion.** Often lost in discussions of leadership is the deep connection to those one leads. Peterson and Seligman referred to this as a sense of humanity, and some of the most powerful forms of leadership have roots in humanity. We interpret it as respect for those one leads and passion for the cause that is grounded in this respect.

- **Courage.** What we see lacking in many leaders is the "fire in their belly" required to lead. Passion and courage are not abstract concepts but rather real manifestations of why an individual wants to lead and what he or she hopes to accomplish. Having courage also acknowledges that leaders face extremely challenging situations in pursuit of their aims. Having persistence and vitality to face obstacles is critical.

- **Transcendence.** Often, achieving greatness requires having a level of aspiration that transcends the obvious. It is a rather rare and interesting collection of character strengths, in the form of hope, humor, gratitude, a sense of spirituality and appreciation of excellence, that appear to foster the capacity to transcend. The challenge, for leaders in many organizations is to appreciate the place for this kind of transcendence. However, apart from religious leaders who embody this quality, like the Dalai Lama, many leaders find the grind of the daily leadership challenge drives out any possibility of transcendence.

When these six virtues are accompanied by the five "intelligences" we have described above, they form the knowledge, understanding, skill, judgment and character required to be a cross-enterprise leader. This is the secret sauce!

Growing and Developing Cross-Enterprise Leaders

How do leaders develop this capability and what can organizations do to stimulate this growth?

We have suggested that BI, SI, OI and PI can be learned. But only part of this, a small part, involves book-based learning or learning in formal executive development programs. PI and OI particularly are learned through critical experiences and reflection on those experiences. You need to try to persuade and influence people to learn how to do it effectively; you need to experience and manage organizational change to learn how to do it well. You need to practice and get feedback and coaching to learn how to be an effective communicator; you need to experience group dynamics to learn how to manage teams for high performance. You need to move yourself outside of your safety zone and experience new challenges, escalating in complexity and the associated risk of failure.

You have to be a constant learner. Almost every minute of every day is an opportunity to deepen these intelligences. While acting to achieve results, leaders have the opportunity to learn and develop. We have a video case series that has become the favorite of many students. It depicts a young leader in Sabena Airlines—the former national airline of Belgium—who faces a series of decisions/actions, most of which take place on the spur of the moment without much time to think or plan. Students realize that it is through this pattern of actions that the organization develops, the strategy unfolds, the business achieves (or fails to achieve) its goals and the leader develops in the process, refining his or her abilities by making the ordinary extraordinary.

It is important to note that developing many of these areas is a pain-free process in that it involves acquiring more intelligence and capability based on the learning experiences arising from day-to-day activities. However, a lot of learning comes from the uncomfortable stretch and difficult experiences that challenge us. While there is opportunity to develop through the ordinary everyday decisions, it is often significant decisions and life experiences that both test us and develop us.

Many leaders look to leadership development programs to accelerate their learning. While this can be achieved, it needs to be recognized that such leadership development is truly a lifelong process. Many leaders and organizations are starting to map that journey, to try and orchestrate the types of experiences that will generate the necessary learning to round out a leader. There is both purpose and happenstance in leadership development and leaders need to embrace both.

Organizations play a vital role in this development. They should be hiring people who are smart and then giving them the critical experiences that are tailored to develop their strengths and weaknesses. We argue that developing strengths alone is insufficient if you want people to have cross-enterprise leadership capabilities. It can be argued that an absence of BI, SI, OI and PI can somehow be compensated for by others in the executive team who may have what one leader lacks. But, in practice, we find this to be rare. The exceptional cross-enterprise leaders that we have seen possess all of the intelligences, though they are neither developed nor manifested to the same degree.

Organizations can make planned interventions when they see that people lack these essential requirements; performance and developmental coaching, coupled with effective mentoring, can be used aggressively to develop strengths and shore-up weaknesses; programs can be used selectively, especially to increase BI and SI; the right kinds of project work and selective assignments can be used to develop OI; internal programs can reinforce the need for these intelligences and help develop them.

Organizations can and must get their executive messaging about this topic right: "Here's what you need to be to get ahead in this organization." And they must manage the credibility associated with this statement; every time a person who lacks PI, for example, is promoted to a senior leadership role, the organization is sending the message that PI doesn't matter.

The hardest thing to develop is an individual's ability to synthesize and deploy the five types of intelligence into a true cross-enterprise leadership capability. Running a business unit, with responsibility for a bottom line, provides a tremendous learning opportunity. A conglomerate or multi-business-unit operation has clear advantages here, because they often have small business units that they can use as training grounds for those that they think have "the right stuff" to be cross-enterprise leaders but who need to be tested and developed further. The availability and use of such challenging opportunities is one of the reasons that companies such as GE have developed so many cross-enterprise leaders. Those companies that lack these opportunities have to create special roles or assignments, rich with the kinds of sequencing and synthesizing challenges that are essential to cross-enterprise leadership development.

The desire for simplicity in both description and prescription has led many authors and researchers to attempt to describe "the great leader" in simple terms. We think that such simple explanations are neither possible nor desirable. For us, leadership—particularly cross-enterprise leadership—always will be an amalgam of character and a multitude of intelligences, with each leader embodying the knowledge, understanding and skills to do the job at hand and plan for the challenges of the future. Those that have these characteristics and who learn to sequence and synthesize them well in a given context will be the effective cross-enterprise leaders of tomorrow.

~4~

Cross-Enterprise Leadership in Practice: An Interview with Turnaround Expert William Aziz

BY GERARD SEIJTS AND MARY CROSSAN WITH BILL AZIZ

There's a certain mystique to the world of turnaround experts—the wizards who descend on an ailing company, perform radical surgery and return it to financial health in short order. But as this conversation with William Aziz makes clear, there's no mystery to the process. Turning a company around means practicing cross-enterprise leadership at the highest level.

Aziz has more than 20 years of turnaround and corporate restructuring experience. He has extensive international experience in multi-party negotiations, strategic partnerships, and merger and acquisition activities. Leading as an executive or a board member, he has been involved in all aspects of balance sheet and operational restructuring in diverse industries, including softwood lumber, steel manufacturing, refrigerated warehousing, transportation, retail, telecommunications, manufacturing and media. Aziz has a reputation for building strong management teams focused on profitability, and promoting strong and flexible thinking to create solutions.

A graduate of the Richard Ivey School of Business at the University of Western Ontario, Aziz is a chartered accountant who spent part of his career with Ernst & Young. He has studied negotiation and multi-party dispute resolution at Harvard Law School and has completed the Institute of Corporate Directors Governance College at the Rotman School of Business at the University of Toronto. He is a director of the Ontario Municipal Employees Retirement System (OMERS) and Canada Bread, and is currently providing his services as CRO of Hollinger Inc. during its restructuring.

The questions in this interview were based on the two cross-enterprise leadership chapters featured in this book: "Cross-Enterprise Leadership: A New Approach for the 21st Century" (chapter 1) and "The Cross-Enterprise Leader" (chapter 3).

Among the key points that emerged from our conversation are the following:

- Being a turnaround expert is like juggling with chainsaws! Turnaround experts must be skilled cross-enterprise leaders.
- Turnaround experts need to understand the business challenges from all angles, not just from one functional perspective such as operations or finance. On the other hand, they must be willing to drill down and understand the business at a deep level.
- Turnaround experts must be comfortable dealing with ambiguity, uncertainty, complexity and time pressures.

- Turnaround experts need to manage the interests of multiple constituencies, and therefore need exceptional interpersonal, networking and collaborative skills.
- Turnaround experts rely on distributed leadership to get things done in an effective and efficient manner. The top-down approach has limitations. People are more likely to take ownership of solutions they helped develop.
- Turnaround experts must have strong strategic skills and a good grasp of the financial aspects of the business.
- Turnaround experts have to be prepared to make tough decisions based on the best information available, and in the best interests of the company.
- Character is critical to achieving turnaround success.
- The Seven Deadly Sins help explain the recent financial crisis.
- Business schools can support the development of leaders by teaching them the courage, conviction and independence of thought to operate in complex business environments.

What does a turnaround expert do? What is the objective of the engagement with an organization?

The principal objective is the restoration of value. There has usually been some cataclysmic event or series of events that has led to deterioration in market position or financial position. It could be a disruptive technology. It could be a loss of confidence—either between major customers and the company in the case of a product that has gone bad, or between major stakeholders such as lenders, bondholders and the company. Typically, the turnaround manager is focused on restoring or normalizing those relationships, enhancing them and re-establishing trust.

The job is a tough one. What motivates you to be a turnaround expert?

It's a complicated answer. I have always had a need to make things better and to help others. I'm never just satisfied with "Okay, I've done that, now I don't have to do anything more." I'm pretty driven that way. I'm also quite competitive and I hate to lose. And I love to create something out of pieces that are broken—it's like solving a jigsaw puzzle. Restructuring and change management give me an opportunity to take companies that have been totally damaged, dismantled or destroyed and rebuild them, often in situations where other people have already tried a lot of solutions. I get the opportunity to be innovative.

I've likened my job to juggling running chainsaws—you come to work every day and hope you don't lose an arm or a leg. I've also said that it's like being the captain of a giant ocean liner trying to turn the ship around. You strap yourself to the tiller and push hard. Eventually you get more people to push with you, because they see you're going to succeed in turning the ship.

I get a great deal of satisfaction from finding solutions and moving people from an entrenched position to consensus or at least to a somewhat agreed-upon position. In many restructuring situations, a good solution is where everybody's a little upset and nobody feels they've really clobbered anyone.

In what ways has the job changed since the financial crisis?

A fundamental change has happened. There's a move toward private resolution or alternative dispute resolution and away from public forum resolution, where possible. Many difficult situations are rebuilt in a consensual forum rather than being jammed down people's throats. There is a lot more ingenuity about how balance sheets are structured. And there's a significant trend toward trying to make the balance sheets more stable and less vulnerable to short-term downturns.

Many businesses have taken a preservation of capital stance because of the uncertainty and rapid rate of change, which has made prediction of currencies, commodities and markets very difficult. Risk assessment and management are fundamental and no longer an afterthought.

From my perspective the arena in which turnaround people work has become much shorter and more focused on the medium term, although there's always the intention to build a stable organization for the long term. Today, you have to have your hands on the controls and never leave things on autopilot.

So how do these developments affect your job?

Beginning back with Enron and the introduction of the *Sarbanes-Oxley Act* and the Ontario equivalent, *Bill 198*, the focus on good governance has led to a greater role for boards of directors in times of crisis or significant change. In the past boards were more likely to take a "hands off, step back and let the new guy do what he has to do" attitude.

Today, there's a lot more reporting required. Directors and senior officers need to be much more in touch with the turn-around manager because of their fiduciary responsibilities. It's not just "come in and be the cowboy with the chainsaw." Now we have an accountability continuum.

How relevant is the cross-enterprise leadership perspective to turnarounds?

It's huge. It's everything, I think. One of the things I learned early on in turning businesses around was that the old model of management—"silo-ing" people along functional disciplines, without even management meetings to hear what was going on in other areas—meant that people were making decisions in a void. Cross-enterprise leadership is the only practical way, the only smart way to run a business.

The principle can be applied at many different levels throughout an organization. It can be part of succession planning and training, with the result that employees can move within the organization with some comfort and knowledge of other areas. You never get caught short because someone quits, becomes ill or wants to take a holiday.

The ability to understand and integrate decision-making and analysis across all disciplines is more about general management and less about becoming a functional specialist. There are and always will be functional specialists within management groups. But leading cross-enterprise change is like a game of "Whac-A-Mole." While you're solving a problem in one area you have to be attuned to where the next one is going to pop up.

Issues may present first in marketing, with consequences in finance or perhaps in a different country that's part of your organization. The resulting cross-enterprise vetting of problems by team members with different perspectives is a positive thing when considering as many of the implications of any decision as possible. Even though you may not get it right 100 percent of the time, at least people will understand more, raise critical issues and do more digging before making a decision.

How do you become a cross-enterprise leader?

I think that cross-enterprise leaders are by nature people who need to understand how things work at a very granular level. Leaders can't lead across an enterprise without understanding what goes on in the enterprise. When I served on a board in the United States the CEO used to call me the "Why Why Guy," because on significant issues I kept drilling to understand more. People who drill into the functions in the organization can then use their skills and knowledge to understand how a decision in one area might impact another. If your style is collaborative and you have a good management team, you lead or influence others to think that way, too.

The cross-enterprise leader is someone who fundamentally wants to understand how a business works and why. That can lead to rethinking and tearing down many things that are done just because they've been done that way for a long time.

What are the core skills that help determine whether a person can succeed as a turnaround expert?

It's all about leadership. Leadership is the ability to influence the way people think or act and to make them follow you in implementing plans to achieve strategic objectives. You don't want people to just blindly follow you: You want them to think about it as they go.

I call the set of skills a turnaround expert uses the golf clubs you have accumulated. You can play 18 holes with a couple of clubs, but the more clubs you have in your bag, the better your game will be. Someone who has only ever done one thing will have trouble being at the top of the chain in making cross-enterprise decisions.

One of the realities about making decisions in restructuring is that you have very compressed time frames, and you often don't have perfect information. So if you're someone who needs 90 percent confidence in the available information in order to make a decision, you won't like restructuring. With restructuring, if you've got 50 percent or 60 percent confidence in the information and you have to make a decision, you get on with it and you don't look back.

You have to be able to think strategically. That doesn't mean that you have to do it alone, but you have to be able to help create flexible solutions to problems. Nothing is static—everything evolves.

You have to encourage people to think laterally, and that is part of their development curve. You have to let them know that it's not a problem if they make a mistake. I'll use a skiing metaphor: If you don't fall down once in a while, you're not skiing hard enough. It's okay to make mistakes—it's how you recover from the mistakes that makes the difference.

Don't mistake tactics for strategy. You would not believe the number of people who think that day-to-day tactics are strategy. They are not. Tactics feed and support strategic initiatives.

You must have some interpersonal skills for this job. If you are a very shy person, or don't like to deal with different types of personalities, you won't be a great leader in a large organization. That's not to say you can't be a leader—you might be a great leader in a research environment or somewhere that requires less personal interaction. It's just that for the type of things I do, it won't work.

You also have to have job knowledge—more golf clubs—and experience working with experts, so you can understand and evaluate what people are telling you.

What would you consider are your strengths as a turnaround expert?

People and finance are my most comfortable and best skills. In my business so much revolves around understanding the money side of things—the profitability and financing elements. That should be second nature to you.

I have to remind myself regularly not to dictate solutions, but instead to let people develop them themselves. Some of that is dictated by the time we have to deal with an issue, but I believe that people need to grow.

If people are allowed to develop something on their own, they cling to it very tightly and they work hard to achieve it. If you delegate solution development rather than dictating it, people can come a long way even in very compressed time frames.

What is the latest thing you've learned or a lesson that you were reminded of?

Things are not always as they appear to be, even if you think you have good information. If you stand close to something, figuratively or literally, it may appear to be something it's not. It may look like a wall—a roadblock in terms of change management—but I have learned to step back and assess what is often a three-dimensional object that can reveal many paths to change. Once you are skilled at seeing this, you find that the cube can be turned inside-out to reveal further options or solutions.

What is the role of character in turnarounds? For example, how do you engage the people that will be at the other end of the change?

I try to engage people eye to eye. You can tell a lot about a person—whether they are being forthright with you—by their body language and whether they look you straight in the eye. In terms of restructuring, I try to get in front of all the constituents as soon as possible. Not by phone, not by e-mail. I think people are drowning in e-mail these days and messages are lost.

My approach is to be honest, and I expect honesty in return. I believe in people until they are dishonest with me. There are always some people who will try to play the system. I try to take the high road.

I always want to understand what people do. Here's an example. When I was President of Interlink Freight Systems, I would go to the docks at 2 a.m. or 3 a.m. I saw what was going on in the warehouse. I rode trucks with drivers through the night. And that helped me to realize that the cause of frustration might be something as simple as a rattle in the truck. The driver would say, "You know, I've asked them to fix that four or five times." I could see that if you sat in there for eight hours with something rattling in your ear, you could come out a crazed animal.

One time I got out of the truck in Montreal and I was just wearing jeans. I wandered into the cafeteria—way before *Undercover Boss*! Our Montreal terminal at the time had a lot of bikers who drove trucks during the day. I sat down and had some bacon and eggs. A driver came over and he said, "Who are you?" I said, "I'm Bill. Who are you?" He sat down, and the next thing you know, I had 100 people around me, and we were talking. It was very informal. I didn't go to the executive offices and put my feet up on the desk. I went downstairs—I talked to people. It turned out to be a good thing. The ability to move between the warehouse floor or a manufacturing facility and the boardroom gives you the ability to reach your audience without talking down to anyone. It's the ability to migrate your personality a little bit—to understand or be compassionate about what people want.

I have a story from the beginning of the Agnew Footwear chain. My predecessor as president was a man named Janci. I stood in the crowd when they were announcing my appointment to replace him. I was beside two women who were chatting and the one woman said—and this is a lasting lesson for me—she said, "Do you think Mr. Janci will come back and say goodbye to us?" The other woman replied, "Why would he? He never said hello!"

It's all about presence. A lot of executives use a back door or come in through their private garage or come up the back stairs and disappear into their office and are totally absorbed with their world. Never do that. Come in through the front door in the morning and say hi to everyone. They'll know when you're in a bad mood too, but don't cut people off. If you put it out that you're approachable, people will come to your office door. They'll feel comfortable enough to come and say, "Hey, I was thinking about something." Eat in the cafeteria once in a while— you don't have to go to a big restaurant every time for lunch.

You really engage with people. Where does that approach come from?

My brothers and sisters would say we get that from our mother. She would talk to anyone. We were brought up in a very engaging environment where everyone talked. You brought your friends home and you talked. It's easy for me to sit down and talk. I was a guest speaker in your class, and some of your former students still call me. There is one person who writes me every month. Every month! I still talk to him—I don't blow him off. He asked me to meet somebody last week. I'm going to meet the person. It's just my style.

A lot of that comes from a fundamental belief that people want to do the right thing. I'm willing to let people prove to me that they want to do the right thing or that they don't. I try not to pre-judge any person or any situation. I try to get as much information as possible. It's somewhat self-serving. If I'm adversarial with you from the start, you're not going to tell me anything. In fact, you might even mislead me, whereas if I'm open and honest, and you can engage me eye to eye, then I can earn your trust and you can tell me what you think.

When I start running a business I declare an amnesty period. The general amnesty allows people to speak frankly about things that they think are wrong. They're not always right because they may not have full information, but it starts a dialogue.

I imagine that businesses often can't be fixed without significant cost cutting. How do you reconcile that with the personal relationships you have established?

Significant change, including cost cutting, is almost always required. If you have a heart at all it is difficult to make those decisions once you connect with people. But I'll give you a personal maxim that I use. You go to work every day and say to yourself, "It's them or it's me." If you don't fix the company, you're going to be gone and there won't be a company. As Mr. Spock said, "The needs of many outweigh the needs of the few."

Yes, some people will lose their jobs, and you try to be as compassionate as you can. I pulled myself through a keyhole at Agnew Footwear the first time I laid off a huge number of people. I did it in late January, so Christmas had just passed and people had bills coming in. It was terrible. I met with every one of them face-to-face and told them myself, which had huge stress attached to it. But I told them. I looked them in the eye and I said, "I hate to do this, but I've got to do it." You can't do that all the time, especially in large organizations. It's a very tough road and sometimes you just have to bite the bullet. Too many executives hope they will not have to deal with this. They wait too long, hoping for a positive change just around the bend.

What leadership lessons would you share with CEOs based on the things that you've seen during the turnarounds?

Number one on my list is focus on execution. Many people can make great plans on a piece of paper. You hear people say, "Well, that's a nice MBA report but can you execute on it?" Business schools teach you how to analyze and produce very pretty, thorough reports, but they don't necessarily lead to execution of what's in the report. That's number one.

Number two would be to focus on a manageable number of objectives. Too many people spread their organizations too thin trying to do too many things. There has to be some kind of analysis and thought put into questions like "What are we going to work on?" "What is the marginal benefit of each of these initiatives?" and "What's the probability of success for each one?" If you can answer those questions, you can decide to do the top three and not the bottom six. You have to start with a really good understanding of what you're trying to achieve.

And the third thing I would say is that too many organizations confuse tactics for strategy. They don't really think strategically. They don't think about how they can differentiate themselves from their competitors—how their company and its products or services are differentiated in the minds of their customers when compared to their competitors. The strategies that lead to that—innovation, satisfaction of customer need, other factors that differentiate you from existing products—need to be a focus.

Too many organizations are worried about whether they can get a product from A to B for five cents less. That's part of it, but it doesn't matter if your product is getting from A to B unless it's different from the product the guy at C is producing. For example, in the steel industry, ArcelorMittal Dofasco and Stelco are in Hamilton and Essar Steel Algoma Inc. is in Sault Ste. Marie. They're all producing steel, but Algoma's got to bring it from Sault Ste. Marie to Hamilton. The company could focus on the cost of transportation, but in my view they should focus on how to build a product that's really needed by customers, that has value added, that differentiates them, that makes them strategic in some way. In the commodity business that may not always be possible, but certainly in most businesses executives have to think about that.

How did you learn to deal with so much uncertainty in your work?

It's a lot like crossing the street. When you're young and you haven't done it a lot, you're nervous. As you cross more and more streets and wider streets you're comfortable doing it. Then you can move to streets where cars are moving faster and you can judge the speed and distance. This type of decision-making is something that develops over time. It's part of the reason why the people who hold themselves out to be restructuring people but haven't really held the reins try to cross the street and get smushed. From both sides!

And the issue of complexity?

Some of it is experience; some of it is capacity to retain. I've always had a great capacity to retain information once I've read it. I don't have a photographic memory or anything, but I have a good memory. To me it's about the ability to connect the dots even though they may not appear all in the same place. And to build a story that makes sense out of connecting those dots. In the end, complexity can usually be broken down into some fundamental pieces. If taken as a whole the situation looks overwhelming, but once you understand the pieces and how they connect, it's usually not as complicated as you thought.

How have you grown as a leader? How has your approach changed over the years?

There has definitely been an evolution. I started out as a "shoot first, ask questions later" guy. I thought I knew more than I did. This goes back to learning from your experiences. I have learned to listen a lot more, to be less judgmental on short notice and to hear more than one side of a story. I guess you could call that maturity.

I've had a couple of fantastic mentors over the years. They are calm, thoughtful and decisive types. I am indebted to them. You could also say that experience has made me a better decision maker. When you make decisions without probing, without information, there's a higher probability of error. There's also less likelihood that you've considered everything that could happen. You may create another crisis that you didn't intend. As a result, I've become more inclusive as time has gone by. I've always been inclusive in terms of decision-making, but now I'm less quick to cut people off and go on to the next thing. A lot less.

Can you please explain the notion of the Seven Deadly Sins that you talked about in the Leadership on Trial[1] initiative?

I have said that the Seven Deadly Sins are very informative in understanding what was happening in the lead-up to the [recent financial] crisis. *Lust* is effectively unrestrained excess. Think of the platform consolidations as businesses were gobbled up by one another. The debt was mounting: You could buy a business and put 90 percent of the purchase price on the balance sheet in debt. It was totally unrestrained. *Gluttony* is continuing to gulp down to the point of waste. Look at the significant acquisitions made by companies like MGM Mirage in the United States and Intrawest in Canada. These acquisitions were financed with debt, and these businesses continued to swallow up other businesses to the point of bursting at the seams. *Greed*—we all know what greed is. It manifested itself in situations like Bernie Madoff, Enron and the number of Ponzi schemes that are out there. *Sloth* is essentially being lazy, not doing your homework, not doing the due diligence required and being encouraged to do just about anything. I can tell you a little story. I was doing a restructuring with a large number of hedge funds involved. The person responsible at one of the lead hedge funds called to discuss an upcoming "all-hands" call. This person said to me, "I'm going to be on the call on Friday but don't ask me any questions." I said, "Okay, didn't you get a chance to read the materials?" He said, "Yeah, yeah, I read everything you sent to me." I said, "Well, okay, why not any questions?" He said,

---

1 Jeffrey Gandz, Mary Crossan, Gerard Seijts, Carol Stephenson and Daina Mazutis, along with a select assembly of diverse leaders from the public and private sector, engaged in an intensive exchange of ideas and insights, delving into the leadership issues exposed by the economic crisis of the past year. The objective was simple: Current economic recovery initiatives, while necessary and laudable, will only serve to deepen and delay a future collapse if not simultaneously supported by real efforts to understand the leadership and organizational issues that cut across industries and borders and lead to these recurrent crises. Chapter 10 provides an article detailing the findings and implications of the Leadership on Trial initiative.

"Well, you're going to be on the speakerphone. It's Friday, and we have our poker game in the office. I don't want anybody to hear we're playing poker during the call." It was incredible—by not using their talents appropriately they were potentially going to affect something very important, and at a critical juncture. *Wrath* is the vehement denial of the truth. Leading up to the crisis it was all about the "rose-colored glasses"—people continuing to believe that they were doing something that wasn't going to cause a problem. *Envy*, the desire for someone else's traits or status or abilities, was everywhere. It was rampant, and I can't say it's gone. People feel like that all the time, and some of it is related to money, to status, and to how you're perceived in the marketplace. And finally, *pride*. It's that feeling of overconfidence people had, the feeling that they were invincible.

How can business schools better prepare their students—executives included—to deal with the kinds of challenges that we have seen in the last couple of years?

Help them to develop conviction, courage and independent thought. People have to be able to follow their own path. I'll give you an example. I'm a director at OMERS, one of Canada's largest pension plans. I'm Vice-Chair of the Investment Committee, and we have $50 billion invested. Yesterday we released our results and we have a 10.6 percent return, which is pretty decent. We need 6.5 percent to pay pensions of the 400,000 firefighters, police and municipal employees who rely on us to manage that pension money.

In the second quarter of 2008, the head of the Capital Markets Group said, "I don't feel good about this marketplace, and I want to take a preservation-of-capital stance." We took $5 billion out of the capital markets and put it in real return bonds.

Nobody else was doing that. There were a lot of questions about whether it was the right thing to do. It was a very conservative move, so coming forward to yesterday, we announce a 10.6 percent return, while other funds maybe have 14 percent or 15 percent, and the really wild ones that bet on the recovery of the market got 25 percent or 30 percent. We didn't get huge gains, and some people may be critical of that. The independent thought was, "We've got to do what's right for us. We've got some very smart people looking at this. We've got to think it through and then take a stand. Let's make our own decision."

OMERS didn't get involved in asset-backed commercial paper because we couldn't understand who was going to be on the hook at the end of the day. Same with credit default swaps. One of the things students should take away from business school is this: Don't endorse anything you don't understand. You have to understand everything you're doing, and if you don't, just keep drilling into it. Do what you believe is the right thing. Exercise independent thought.

Can you reflect on your career thus far and articulate your personal leadership brand?

I'd like to be able to brandish the U.S. Marines motto, "The Few. The Proud. The Brave." It personifies what I do. I have to be true to myself. In other words, I don't compromise myself or my beliefs. That's very important to me. Second, I must be honest with other people. The delivery of a message can make a difference but in the end you just need to be honest. Don't try to cloud things or butter it up in any way. Third, my brand is analytical. I make sure that I understand everything so I don't repeat others' mistakes. Otherwise you're destined to repeat history. Fourth, I don't try to do everything myself.

You can't be everything to everyone, so know when you need resources and make sure that you understand your short-comings and fill the gaps with help. I have found some true "diamonds in the rough" among those I have worked with, and they have gone on to have great careers. Finally, I believe in thanking people for doing a good job. Make sure that you acknowledge when people have done something of value.

Any final thoughts?

I've always been very proud that I took what I learned at business school and tried to make the people who taught me proud. And I've kept those connections. (Ivey Professor) Jim Erskine and I are still friends. He's someone I think of as a truly great builder of business leaders. I call him the man with the arrows. He used to mark exams with an arrow as opposed to a mark. At 12 o'clock you were doing great. At 3 okay. Below 3 o'clock you were not passing. His influence in not judging things by conventional standards was unusual but effective in resetting our expectations and adjudicating progress. Jim showed us critical thinking in a way that was easily understood. I try to apply that in my work. John Nicholson, head of the HBA program in my day, was a very influential guy too. Their influence is among the reasons I give back by speaking with Ivey students every year.

~5~

Driving Growth through Entrepreneurship and Innovation

BY SIMON C. PARKER

Cross-enterprise leaders need to be able to look beyond specific functions such as finance, marketing or operations to tackle issues that span the entire enterprise—issues like growth, innovation, productivity and globalization. And they must understand how every part of the business fits into a complex business environment. This, of course, is exactly how successful entrepreneurs have always worked, and explains the role of the Driving Growth Through Entrepreneurship & Innovation (DGEI) Research Centre in the cross-enterprise leadership initiative, launched by Ivey in September 2005.

Cross-enterprise leadership is a revolutionary departure from conventional approaches to business education, which have traditionally divided management and learning into functional disciplines. Instead of hearing about marketing in one class and finance in another, Ivey students learn to think, act and lead universally and flexibly through a set of sequential, yet integrated, modules. With cross-enterprise leadership, Ivey has responded to the urgent need for leaders who can guide organizations through today's complex, sometimes treacherous and increasingly global environment.

This chapter makes the case that effective entrepreneurship embodies several key aspects of cross-enterprise in practice. The chapter comprises several examples of cross-enterprise thought leadership conducted by members of the DGEI in recent years. Each example presents some of the intricate environments encountered in entrepreneurship and the cross-enterprise lessons that can be distilled from them. The final section closes by summarizing the relationship between entrepreneurship and cross-enterprise leadership.

Been There, Done That

This section profiles the research of DGEI member and Ivey Professor Claus Rerup, who explains why past experience as an entrepreneur is no guarantee of future success. In this example, Rerup emphasizes the notion of mindfulness, which reflects the importance and criticality of attention, particularly in settings where failures can be catastrophic. Cross-enterprise leaders, while they need to have a holistic appreciation of the enterprise, also must be mindful of organizational routines and habits, especially when these are no longer serving the purpose they once did. Furthermore, cross-enterprise leaders, as experienced as they might be, can't afford to always blindly follow personal experience but must possess the wisdom to reflect and reassess when necessary.

A good example that illustrates some of the issues involved is Stelios Haji-Ioannou. Stelios (he prefers to be called by his first name) founded his first company, Stelmar Shipping, at the ripe old age of 25. His biggest success story to date, easyJet, changed the face of aviation in Europe in a matter of just a few years. By the age of 38, he had established more than 15 ventures, including an oil tanker business that sold in 2005 for $1.3 billion. Today, Stelios sees himself as the manager of a brand that has been extended into industries such as travel, leisure, telecom and personal finance.

It is natural to assume that Stelios' success is due to his experience as an entrepreneur. After all, we've all been told that experience is a good teacher. But Rerup believes benefiting from experience may be more complex than we assume. "The more I read and understood about experience," says Rerup, "the more I realized that things were not that simple." He noticed, for example, that some habitual entrepreneurs—those who start several businesses and often operate two or more at the same time—were able to replicate their initial successes fairly consistently in a variety of ventures, while others clearly couldn't.

So how do habitual entrepreneurs (HEs) use past entrepreneurial experiences to positively affect future ventures? That's the question Rerup has addressed in his research designed to question received wisdom and explore new concepts. His conclusions contain some food for thought for entrepreneurs looking to benefit from their past experience.

Previous researchers have generally assumed that habitual entrepreneurs like Stelios are successful simply because they draw on their experience. Yet empirical evidence doesn't bear this idea out, showing no definitive positive relationship between HEs' previous start-up experience and the performance of their businesses. Some research even suggests that when HEs take on new ventures that are unrelated to prior businesses, they are more likely to be successful than when the new venture is in a related industry.

To illustrate the pitfalls of experience, Rerup considered the potential negative and positive impacts of different types of experience on the two core activities of entrepreneurship— opportunity discovery and opportunity exploitation. For example, he noted that prior success in a business might help by encouraging the habitual entrepreneur to continue good practices. On the other hand, it might lead her to oversimplify the challenges of the new business, get into "cognitive and behavioral ruts," and become overconfident. Similarly, experience in the same industry might give the HE useful knowledge about how to operate the new business, but might also encourage him to use routines and business models that don't apply in a different situation.

Rerup finds the concept of *mindfulness* useful in separating experience that benefits and harms a new venture. The concept was developed by psychologist Ellen Langer to explain aspects of individual behavior. In its simplest terms, mindfulness is about paying attention. "It's very much about the *quality* of attention," Rerup notes. "And it's also about what you do with what you attend to. Mindfulness is not just about cognition—it's also about action." When people apply experience with mindfulness, they differentiate experience, adapt it to new contexts and use it creatively. Mindless behavior, in contrast, is marked by blind, rigid application of experience. It has been described as "being on automatic pilot."

The concept of mindfulness has been applied to organizations, especially so-called High Reliability Organizations— nuclear plants, chemical plants and other organizations that can't afford errors because they operate high-risk technologies.

Researchers have identified five subprocesses that operational-
ize mindfulness in these organizations: pre-occupation with
failure, reluctance to simplify interpretations, sensitivity to
operations, commitment to resilience and under-specification
of structure. Naturally, counterparts to these subprocesses can
be readily found in cross-enterprise leadership in "real-world"
entrepreneurship.

At first glance, mindfulness appears to be the answer to using
experience beneficially. It seems logical that the more mindful an
entrepreneur is, the more likely he is to succeed. But once again,
Rerup argues it isn't that simple. "You don't get mindfulness for
free, and it often falls apart because it's very, very difficult to be
mindful all the time." Mindfulness often requires an investment
of time and people and an ongoing effort to sustain and rebuild.
Sometimes using past experience mindlessly—a sort of "just do
it" approach—can produce good results.

When he compares the five subprocesses of mindfulness in
High Reliability Organizations to the activities of entrepreneurship, he again gets mixed results. For example, "pre-occupation
with failure" might help entrepreneurs by making them more
realistic and cautious. On the other hand, it could serve to
undermine optimism and action. Similarly, "sensitivity to operations" can help entrepreneurs anticipate problems early on,
but also can lead to information overload and scattered focus.

Rerup suggests a new model, one that recognizes both the
benefits and pitfalls of using experience in mindful or mindless
ways. When a business venture and its context are complex,
dynamic, ambiguous and unpredictable, he suggests the benefits of mindfulness may outweigh its costs. In less complex,
more static situations, mindfulness is not as important, and the
economics of mindlessness are more appropriate.

Stelios is a case in point. "Stelios is quite mindful about how his prior experience can both help and hurt his new ventures," Rerup says. "He seems to have found ways to balance the costs and benefits of each type of prior experience." For example, he uses his status and brand to build relationships and identify new markets, but he also adapts past lessons to each new business. By treating every business as distinct, he avoids the trap of taking too much for granted. Yet he also uses his prior industry experience to get new ventures up and running. The differences between some ventures keep him thoughtful and prevent him from blindly replicating the past, yet his experience as a maverick drives innovation in a variety of industries. He is careful not to overextend his brand and turns down more ideas than he sponsors.

Do other habitual entrepreneurs demonstrate a similar combination of mindful and mindless application of experience? Rerup says the way to answer this question is to follow several HEs over a period of time, to see when they succeed, when they fail and how they use their experience mindfully or mindlessly in each situation. In such a study, it would be important to have a stratified sample of businesses, including some very simple examples, like restaurants and construction companies, and some more complex ones, like airlines and telecommunications businesses. "As educators and advisors to entrepreneurs, we need to understand if knowledge gained about mindfulness in High Reliability Organizations can be applied to entrepreneurship," says Rerup. "If we can help even 10 percent to 15 percent of habitual entrepreneurs be more successful the second or third time around, we could have a huge impact on the economy."

In the meantime, he says entrepreneurs may be able to help themselves by thinking about the ideas he raises and asking how

they apply to their ventures. If they are operating complex businesses in dynamic industries, taking the time and trouble to be
mindful about past experience may pay dividends. On the other
hand, it may sometimes make sense to apply past experience
mindlessly, simply repeating behaviors that resulted in success
in the past. "Generating research takes years and years," he points
out. "Until then, these ideas may provide some useful tools—a
way of thinking that will help entrepreneurs in the operational
phase of their venture. Why not at least be *mindful* that being
mindful can have both advantages and disadvantages?" In the
light of these arguments, it would seem that cross-enterprise leadership that emphasizes mindfulness will be of great practical value
to entrepreneurs in the day-to-day running of their ventures.

Think "How"

This section profiles the research of Ivey Professors Mark
Vandenbosch and Niraj Dawar, who challenge entrepreneurial companies to realize the value in customer relations. While
many businesses push a single-minded agenda of better, faster
and more innovative products, Vandenbosch and Dawar highlight the always fundamental importance of being able to create
value for customers and to solve their problems. It can be a
lengthy and challenging task to build the necessary relationships and earn the respect and trust of customers. However,
cross-enterprise leaders are particularly suited for this task given
their focus on "big picture" views of the enterprise (what do we
know?) and leveraging knowledge about customers' businesses
(how do we use it?) for competitive advantage.

   Ralph Waldo Emerson coined the famous phrase that once
seemed to capture the essence of entrepreneurship: "Build

a better mousetrap and the world will beat a path to your door." Trouble is, Emerson lived in the mid-19th century when mousetraps, and indeed all technologies, moved slower than they do today. Hence Vandenbosch and Dawar quickly came to the realization that Emerson's phrase is no longer a guide to business success. "Pretty much any product anyone makes can be copied very quickly," says Vandenbosch. "The increasingly rapid and free flow of information, the movement to global standards and the advent of open markets for components and technologies have tended to equalize companies' abilities to innovate."

So if competitors can easily duplicate your clever mousetrap, how do you create sustainable competitive advantage? That's the question Vandenbosch and Dawar have been exploring. They believe the answer lies in going beyond better products to capture the value in customer interactions.

Vandenbosch and Dawar have interviewed close to 2,000 senior managers in both large and small companies across a wide range of industries. They asked the simple question, "Why do your customers buy from you rather than from your competitors?" The answer came back loud and clear. Although great products and technologies are the entry stakes, factors such as trust, confidence, convenience, product support and ease of doing business are what really make the difference.

"There is no doubt that great products, services and technologies—the 'what'—are essential to creating customer value," Vandenbosch says. "But we believe that customers derive as much, if not more, value from *how* they interact with the seller." Entrepreneurs may have a tendency to depend more heavily on their product or technology concept, but Vandenbosch says that's not wise in the long run. "People rely on good old

R&D to come up with the better mousetrap, but focusing on product innovation only puts your company on an ever faster competitive treadmill."

The two researchers believe that value can be created by focusing on two aspects of customer interaction—lowering costs and reducing risk. "Ultimately what really matters is that you are solving problems for your customers," says Vandenbosch.

A company can lower costs for its customers by, for example, taking on functions that are similar across its customer base. Master Builders, a company that sells chemical admixtures used to improve the performance of concrete, developed a remote tank-monitoring system so that customers would always have the supplies they needed without delay or extra cost. Orica, an Australian multinational in the commercial explosives business, moved from supplying explosives to taking charge of the entire blast and offering customers contracts for "broken rock."

Computer maker Dell takes a different approach. It integrates with client IT departments, simplifying the order process, eliminating setup and delivery expenses by preloading customized software, and improving maintenance through remote monitoring and extensive e-service. As a result, customers have reorganized and in some cases reduced their purchasing, accounting and IT investment.

Vandenbosch and Dawar say there is significant potential value in what they call the "Seller's Hidden Advantage." Because of their birds-eye perspective, sellers often know things about their customers' businesses that customers don't know. "As a seller you deal with a network of customers," says Vandenbosch. "If you leverage that network, you can develop valuable knowledge and expertise." Whether you deal with many customers in one industry, or do similar work for customers in a wide range of industries, there are opportunities to acquire and share valuable knowledge. For example, Hilti Corp., a maker of high-end power tools and fastening systems, operates as an information network, solving problems for customers in one place by using experience gained elsewhere in their worldwide network of customers. "Hilti and its customers consider its customer orientation, application know-how, and advisory skills to be strengths that justify its premier prices," says Vandenbosch. Among ways to realize the Seller's Hidden Advantage are these:

- Relay valuable experience gained through other interactions to solve thorny problems for your customers.
- Create benchmarks for customers, showing them where they stand in comparison with peers and helping them improve their position.
- Bring together disparate pieces of information about a customer's business and interpret their meaning to add value.

Innovative solutions like these lead to more interwoven interactions with customers, making it more difficult for competitors to come between you. In the case of Dell, for example, many customers have been able to reduce the size of their IT staffs because of the services Dell offers. They are willing to do so because the savings more than compensate them for the extra risk of tying themselves to a specific seller. "By willingly intermeshing with Dell, customers make relationship-specific investments—or in this case, disinvestments—that make them less likely to buy from Dell's competitors."

Of course, finding innovative solutions that cut across traditional disciplinary and functional boundaries is the essence of cross-enterprise thinking. But building value through customer relations isn't the road to overnight success: It takes time to build strong relationships and earn the respect and trust of customers. For entrepreneurs with a hot new product, that can be frustrating. "They know their product is better, so they don't understand why nobody is buying it," says Vandenbosch. "The fact is, you still have to earn it. No matter what your strategy, something new is always risky." Success from "how"-based innovation takes time to realize, but once achieved, is more difficult to imitate and easier to sustain. Perhaps entrepreneurs would be better served by another famous quotation from Emerson: "Do not go where the path may lead; go instead where there is no path and leave a trail."

Sooner or Later

This section profiles research by Paul Beamish—Ivey Professor, Director of the Engaging Emerging Markets Research Centre and founding Director of Ivey's Asian Management Institute, and Canada Research Chair in International Business. Beamish observes that more and more entrepreneurial ventures are taking to foreign markets, and finds that it is better not to wait. Entrepreneurs and cross-enterprise leaders pursuing an international strategy need to think carefully about the timing of going global. Careful thinking and strategizing, however, work best with a flexible and fluid form of enterprise management, particularly one with a drive to keep learning. This is exactly the kind of management that cross-enterprise leaders exhibit, especially in the face of time pressure.

When we think of the global environment of business, we often think of giant multinationals whose wealth and power span the world. But this ignores the important and growing role of small and medium-sized entrepreneurial ventures

(SMEs). "Few multinational firms are born large," says Beamish. "Typically, they start off as SMEs."

With increasing numbers of small to mid-size firms looking beyond their domestic markets, international entrepreneurship is becoming an exciting new research theme. Entrepreneurship and international business are two research paths that inevitably intersect: The very act of entering a foreign market involves innovation and risk-taking, both hallmarks of entrepreneurship.

Some new ventures, particularly in e-commerce, are global from the moment they're born. But most international SMEs start off as domestic firms, says Beamish, and then decide to expand. "An unsolicited export order is often the first reason. Others include such things as perceived opportunities and saturated local markets."

Beamish and co-author Jane Lu, of Singapore Management University, recently published a paper, "SME Internationalization and Performance: Growth vs. Profitability," in the *Journal of International Entrepreneurship*. In their paper, Beamish and Lu look at different internationalization strategies and compare their effects on performance. These strategies are exporting and foreign direct investment (FDI). Their successful execution depends on cross-enterprise thinking within the organization and the ability of the organization to mobilize and integrate resources both internally and externally (inside and outside the firm).

The decision to expand into foreign markets is a very important one for a small or mid-size firm. The two most common avenues are exporting and FDI. Both strategies come with different risks and require different organizational structures and capabilities. "A firm should carefully consider its strategic objectives in terms of growth or profit before it decides whether to pursue exporting or FDI," says Beamish.

The distinction between firm growth and profitability is important, says Beamish. "While both goals are common performance metrics, they are not the same thing. The reason we distinguish between different goals is that they require somewhat different actions to be pursued."

Exporting is an easier and less risky strategy than FDI. Exports increase sales, resulting in economies of scale and production efficiencies. They also help firms gain knowledge of overseas markets and new technological capabilities, leading to future FDI. On the other hand, exporting is dependent on overseas government trade regulations and currency exchange rates that can change quickly.

FDI requires more investment and leaves the SME less flexible if it needs to suddenly withdraw from an overseas market. With greater risk, though, comes the opportunity for greater reward. Firms learn a lot about host countries by being on the spot and can gain access to cheaper and newer resources.

Any firm that moves into an international market has a steep learning curve, a disadvantage often referred to in the research literature as the *liabilities of foreignness*. An entrant to a foreign country has little knowledge about local customers and business practices. It also has few, if any, relationships with customers, buyers, suppliers and regulatory bodies. "SMEs can reduce the liabilities of foreignness by partnering with local firms through equity and non-equity alliances or through acquisitions of local firms," says Beamish. "The good news is that these liabilities go away or decline as the SME acquires more experience of operating in the foreign country."

In their study, Beamish and Lu found that exporting and FDI both led to firm growth. The results differed for the Japanese SMEs in the study, though, when the researchers looked at profitability. Exporting, which had a positive impact on firm growth, had a negative impact on profitability. The explanation for this finding may ring true to Canadian exporters in the present: The value of the yen increased significantly during the time period studied. "We can conclude from our study that exporting is an effective growth strategy," says Beamish, "but SMEs must understand that profitability could be weakened or even reversed during periods of currency appreciation." There are ways to mitigate this risk, and SMEs that are dependent upon exporting should explore these options.

FDI, on the other hand, had a positive effect on both growth and profitability. The impact on profitability was U-shaped: Profitability declined in the early stages of FDI, and then improved. "In the initial stages of foreign direct investment, firms may have to pay *tuition* in terms of profits for their foreignness," says Beamish, "but an extended level of FDI is associated with improved profitability."

The reality for most international SMEs is a combination of both exports and FDI. In their study, Beamish and Lu looked at how firms could best configure these activities. They found that a combination of high levels of exporting and FDI led to higher firm growth, but because of greater demands on firm structures and management capabilities, these factors tended to depress profitability.

Another important finding for entrepreneurs is that age has an effect on performance. Beamish and Lu found that SMEs that expand into global markets at a younger age achieve higher growth rates than SMEs who are more established in their domestic market. "The older an SME, the harder it is for it to adapt to new environments and new ways of doing business," says Beamish. "Early internationalizers have not yet developed rigid routines, and are still flexible and able to learn more quickly in international markets."

Interestingly, younger firms who expand into foreign markets do not initially perform as well financially as older ones at the time of their entry. All new ventures face the *liabilities of newness*, a disadvantage that is well documented by existing research. New firms do not enjoy relationships with buyers, customers, suppliers, and governmental and regulatory agencies. Nor do they have the benefit of experience. "The liability of newness can cause these firms to make more mistakes when entering foreign markets, leading to worsened rather than improved financial performance at the early stages of internationalization," says Beamish, "but they learn more quickly to adjust, and those that survive perform better in the long run than their more entrenched peers."

This finding confirms the validity of another proposition of entrepreneurship research, the *learning advantages of newness*. "Newer firms have less rigid ways of conducting business and are more able to learn new ways of doing business," says Beamish. "Hence, newer firms may perform better than older ones in international markets that are 'new' as compared to domestic markets." Part of the reason for this learning advantage can no doubt be found in the simpler organizational structure enjoyed by small entrepreneurial ventures, in which cross-enterprise leadership may arguably be easier to practice.

"Going global is a big step for an entrepreneurial firm but the right strategy helps mitigate the risk," says Beamish. Managers thinking about moving into foreign markets should consider

- their goals in terms of growth or profit
- their risk-taking and investing capabilities
- their sources of competitive advantage

"Growth-oriented firms can use both exporting and FDI, but those that are more risk-averse should consider starting off with exports," says Beamish. "Profit-oriented firms should avoid high levels of both exporting and FDI activities simultaneously." Furthermore, "entrepreneurs should think carefully about timing. Sooner may be better than later, especially if the firm is able to mitigate their liabilities through alliances or partnerships."

In short, cross-enterprise leadership in entrepreneurship exhibits new and special challenges in the context of internationalization. The value of alliances and partnerships, for example, calls for holistic thinking about opportunities that can be exploited outside the venture's usual context. Cross-enterprise thinking can help achieve this, but also help in the challenge of integrating new operations with an international dimension together with the venture's pre-existing operations.

Levers and Buffers

Networking is the manufacturer's secret weapon in the innovation race. In this section, DGEI members and Ivey Professors Oana Branzei and Stewart Thornhill reveal the importance of establishing and maintaining diverse R&D networks. Branzei and Thornhill demonstrate how businesses can apply these external R&D networks with different situational effects. In some cases these networks can act as levers to bolster internal efforts, and in others they can buffer against negative effects. Since cross-enterprise leaders are particularly capable of identifying potential partners, initiating and maintaining relationships, and working collaboratively within a network, this example is especially illustrative of where cross-enterprise leaders can excel.

Nowadays manufacturing processes are technologically complex, regardless of whether the end product is a cardboard box or a circuit board. Firms need to keep up with the latest technology and ensure that their innovative capabilities are matched to industry conditions. "But, firms needn't always rely on expensive, in-house R&D infrastructure; in some cases, forging alliances with external R&D partners can complement, or even substitute for, home-grown capabilities," says Ivey's Branzei.

Branzei and co-author Thornhill have investigated the relationship between innovative capabilities, R&D networks and revenue growth in a large sample of firms in the Canadian manufacturing sector. They found several good reasons for firms to build strong relationships with external R&D partners such as universities, government agencies, industry associations and independent consultants. "But the key point is that diverse R&D networks benefit both industry laggards and industry leaders—although they benefit them in very different ways," says Branzei. Firms that already employ cutting-edge technologies well-suited to their market conditions can leverage this advantage by establishing diverse R&D networks. At the other end of the scale, R&D networks kick-start those firms that have let their innovative capabilities and technologies get out of sync with the market. These networks buffer them from the negative effects of falling behind the eight ball and help them quickly catch up.

One way to assess innovation is to take an honest look at the sets of actions that enable firms to come up with creative ideas and then convert them into reliable, profitable new products.

Branzei and Thornhill looked at how full the glass was and at how firms were filling it. A key indicator of innovative success is the number of new products spun into the market, so Branzei and Thornhill looked at how manufacturers found good ideas and how they converted these knowledge inputs into profitable products. First, firms tend to search for ideas internally or externally—by attending trade fairs, exhibitions, and conferences; using web-based information networks; and working with universities, government agencies and research laboratories. Next, they "absorb" the insights they find by incorporating new materials and technologies into current operational routines, retooling machinery, retraining employees or acquiring new equipment and software.

Branzei and Thornhill used a comprehensive dataset to see how manufacturing firms stacked up against each other in terms of their ability to convert innovation into performance. However, it's no guarantee of success to simply be more innovative than your rivals. Superior performance depends on how closely a firm's internal capabilities match its technological and market requirements. In other words, it's not just *which* capabilities a firm develops, but how well these capabilities *match* the specific competitive setting. "Firms operating in a stable industry should think twice about gearing up a highly innovative R&D department or hiring top scientists. They can tap into the same pool of innovative capabilities more quickly and effectively by partnering for R&D," says Branzei. "But there is no way around intense innovation efforts in fast-moving sectors, like telecommunications or software development."

And here's where diverse R&D networks come into their own: by *leveraging* the positive effects of innovative capabilities that are well-matched to their environment and *buffering* the negative effects of capabilities that are out of sync with the prevailing market conditions.

Firms operating in dynamic environments have to be able to quickly and efficiently convert knowledge into new products. Under these conditions, firms with above-average innovative capabilities are in a better position to detect and act on new technological opportunities. Diverse R&D alliances amplify this advantage because they act as conduits of pseudo-capabilities—that is, capabilities "borrowed" from network partners, which can be bolted-on temporarily when the firm needs to quickly grab a competitive opportunity. Diverse R&D networks allow innovative firms to extract even greater value from their existing capabilities.

As the market stabilizes, innovative capabilities are less important because leaders can preserve their advantage through incremental advances. In these circumstances, diverse R&D alliances can help firms outperform their rivals in two ways. First, R&D networks offer new sources of learning, innovation and market performance for firms that have exhausted the opportunities available within their established technological domains or current market niches. Second, diverse external relationships motivate firms to look beyond the familiar and the proven to find new sources of opportunities. "Second-hand experiences can stimulate new ideas and interpretations, and inspire innovative solutions," says Branzei. "Firms that are stuck with inadequate innovative capabilities can find alternative sources of advantage via their R&D partnerships." In this way, diverse R&D alliances act as a buffer in stable environments. This mitigates the damaging impact of environmentally misaligned innovation capabilities on firm performance.

Turning to lessons for managers, "we found that diverse R&D networks helped firms across a wide range of manufacturing industries achieve above-average levels of growth. Companies with strong R&D networks outperformed their competitors, regardless of the state of their in-house R&D departments or the volatility of their market. However, establishing and maintaining diverse R&D alliances is much more than *just a bit of networking*," says Branzei. "These partnerships are strategic tools for balancing internal capabilities and environmental demands. Networks can compensate for your weaknesses and magnify your strengths. And, the more diverse the network, the stronger the effect." The implications for cross-enterprise leadership should be clear. Networks can compensate for internal limitations by bridging with external partners and stakeholders. Cross-enterprise in this context involves working across enterprises rather than exclusively within them.

Strategic Leadership and Innovation

CEOs often are told that their firms must "innovate or die," but then are left without much direction regarding their personal role in the process. In this section, Ivey Professor Mary Crossan, together with Ivey's Daina Mazutis, investigates the important relationship between strategic leadership and innovation. In particular, Crossan and Mazutis explore the important role that creativity and support for innovation at the management level play in promoting change and new ideas. Thinking creatively and fostering a distributed culture supportive of innovation across the whole enterprise is another important role of a cross-enterprise leader.

In the last decade, it has been almost impossible for managers, entrepreneurs and business owners to escape the almost continuous and ominous warnings by the popular press to either innovate or die. In the last few months alone these words have appeared in headlines related to a broad range of industry sectors, including the broadcasting and newspaper industries, the mail service and even the online dating industry (yes, industry). Business leaders are constantly reminded that "incrementalism is innovation's worst enemy," "the only sustainable competitive advantage comes from out-innovating the competition" and "to cling to outmoded methods ... is a prescription for suicide." In today's dynamic environments, a firm's ability to innovate is therefore touted to be not just an important ingredient for financial success, but also crucial to a company's very prospects for survival.

Globalization, the speed of technological change, perpetual shifts in market demand and increasing consumer power all have placed a premium on a firm's innovative capabilities. However, our understanding of innovation processes, and specifically the relationship between strategic leadership and organizational innovation, remains poorly understood. This can have fairly drastic consequences. For example, 65 percent of senior executives recently surveyed by McKinsey and Co. claimed to be only "somewhat," "a little," or "not at all" confident about the decisions they make with regards to leading innovation in their organizations. Similarly, the general consensus reached in a recent online panel of senior executives conducted by Harvard Business School concluded that "management practice has little to contribute to processes of creation and innovation." These perceptions are disconcerting, considering that there appears to be considerable anecdotal evidence, from the Bill Gateses to the Steve Jobses of this world, to suggest that strategic leadership can in fact make a difference to successful organizational innovation.

To investigate this issue, Crossan and Mazutis engaged in a comprehensive systematic review of the empirical literature on leadership and innovation. To partially assuage the doubts held by some managers or entrepreneurs, they found plenty of evidence that the demographics, personality characteristics and behaviors of senior executives can both directly and indirectly affect organizational innovation at multiple levels.

Numerous studies have linked specific CEO characteristics directly to organizational innovation. "There is a stream of research that has demonstrated that a firm, or the strategic directions taken by the firm, can be seen as a reflection of its top management team," Mazutis says. "For example, younger CEOs are more likely to spend on R&D than are their older counterparts, ostensibly as this relates to individual risk-seeking profiles, which are hypothesized to be more pronounced in younger entrepreneurs." Similarly, top managers with longer firm tenures also are more likely to be committed to the status quo and therefore less likely to make big investments in innovation. In addition, a CEO's education and functional background can play a role in innovative decision-making, with more educated top management teams and those with more marketing or engineering backgrounds being more creatively inclined than less educated CEOs or those that have spent more time in finance or accounting.

Senior executive characteristics, beliefs and behaviors also can affect organizational innovation. "Research has shown that CEO personality traits such as extraversion, openness to experience and agreeableness can positively affect organizational innovation," Crossan says. "CEO attitudes towards innovation and the strategic emphasis they place on innovative activities are also important determinants of success." In terms of leadership behaviors, transformational leadership in particular—in which leaders are able to inspire, influence and motivate their followers as well as show individual consideration and provide employees with intellectual stimulation—seems to be a leadership style particularly well suited for organizational innovation.

As such, it is not enough for senior executives to just passively support innovation, they must also take the lead in removing all obstacles, both big and small, that can get in the way of the process. "There is a strong leadership role in determining what rules should be broken and which rules need to be followed," Crossan emphasizes. "Often it seems like it is the little things that go wrong that can undermine innovative initiatives and these little things might not seem 'big enough' to trouble leaders—but the cumulative effect of the red tape, lack of care and attention, and inefficiency can take its toll on innovation." Essentially, CEOs and other senior executives should look for what saps energy in the organization—as it is these "little things" in particular that can turn out to be innovation killers.

Sometimes the effect of strategic leadership on innovation is therefore less direct. Mazutis asserts that "multiple studies have found that top managers can influence organizational innovation by creating an organizational climate or culture that supports innovation and by encouraging learning and knowledge creation within the firm." Ensuring that project managers at the group level also have the requisite skills needed to foster creativity, such as encouraging initiative and providing support and feedback, is also necessary for organizational innovation, as is creating a structure within the organization that allows for autonomous yet cross-functional team work.

A leader's ability to make a difference in the level of innovation may, however, also be affected by less easily changeable factors, such as the size or location of the firm, available cash from past firm performance or the level of dynamism in the industry. The socio-cultural context also may constrain or enhance a transformational leader's ability to affect organizational innovation. "This makes leading innovation both a reflection of a leader's individual skill and ability as well as an expression of organizational and environmental factors."

Turning to lessons for managers, a review of more than 75 empirical studies showed that organizational innovation is a process that can be perceived to be both driven from the bottom up—from creative individuals and innovation champions within the firm—as well as top down—from leaders at the strategic apex of the organization and their belief in the crucial effects of innovation on firm growth and survival. "Throughout our research, however, we found that the single most important variable shown to be positively associated with innovation at all levels across a multitude of studies was 'managerial support for innovation,'" Mazutis says. "But this must be an active role for management, not a passive one."

Knowing this, senior executives should be careful to display a favorable attitude toward change ensure that they place a visible strategic emphasis on innovation and create a climate that supports the generation, testing and implementation of new ideas. "Perhaps because of a perceived focus on group or unit level processes such as 'new product development' and 'research and development,' some senior executives have been led to believe that their role is simply to stay out of the way of innovation projects, which happen 'somewhere else,'" Crossan warns. "However, entrepreneurs should not make the mistake of delegating the responsibility for innovation to someone else in the organization. They must also understand the role that they personally play in creating and supporting organizational innovation in their companies." Removing the little obstacles that get in the way of innovation is just as important as ensuring that the big systems, structures and policies are in place. The ability to keep an overview of the big picture while attending to numerous detailed problems operating across the different parts of an enterprise evidently calls for smart cross-enterprise leadership skills.

Why Is It Small Firms that Produce the Entrepreneurs?

The answer lies not so much in what small firms do, says Ivey Professor and DGEI Director Simon Parker, but instead in the kind of employees that they attract. Entrepreneurs appear to self-select, that is, individuals who tend to prefer greater flexibility and autonomy find their way to small firms. The dispositions of entrepreneurs tend to mesh well with the characteristics of small firms. Importantly, these individuals tend to be less risk-averse and have a greater willingness to tolerate some uncertainty. Flexibility, understanding risk and a tolerance for uncertainty are all important characteristics of cross-enterprise leadership, suggesting links between how we identify both entrepreneurs and cross-enterprise leaders.

In an episode of *Dragon's Den*, the popular CBC show in which budding entrepreneurs pitch their business ideas to wealthy Canadian financiers, Darrell Bachmann and his wife, Colleen, walked away with a deal for $1 million. Bachmann came up with the idea of golf shoes with retractable metal spikes, giving traction on the fairway while protecting the greens.

A former golf course superintendent in Chilliwack, B.C., Bachmann fits the profile of those who start their own ventures, says Parker. One of Parker's recent studies shows that the great majority of entrepreneurs come from small businesses. "My study shows very convincingly that small firms are much better hothouses for new venture creation than large firms," he says.

Researchers throughout the developed world have come to the same conclusion: Small firms produce a disproportionate number of entrepreneurs. Why is this so? In Parker's study, he advanced three theories: "transmission," "blocked mobility" and "self-selection." To test his theories, he used the British Household Panel Survey (BHPS) to collect data about those who had quit their jobs to start up their own businesses. BHPS is a large and unique study that began in 1991 and follows through time a representative sample of more than 10,000 individuals.

The transmission theory suggests that small firms do a better job than large firms in equipping and preparing their employees to be entrepreneurs, by offering them greater flexibility, autonomy and access to clients. Surprisingly, perhaps, Parker found little support for this theory from the data. "One would expect that access to customers and seeing at close hand how a business fits together would make employees more inclined to start up on their own," he says. "While these conditions may help explain the success of these start-ups, they do not explain why they actually occur in the first place."

The blocked mobility theory rests on an old but persistent notion that large firms offer the really good jobs, with great opportunities for upward mobility, perks, fringe benefits and security. In comparison, jobs with small firms are less secure and remunerative. Employees in small firms become frustrated, and because they are excluded or "blocked" from employment in large firms, they set up their own businesses. Parker found no evidence to support this theory.

Parker found strong evidence, on the other hand, to support the theory of self-selection. This theory is based on the idea that entrepreneurs share certain preferences, and individuals with these preferences are prone to choose employment in small firms. These individuals tend to prefer the greater flexibility, autonomy and flatter structures offered by small firms, and are not put off by lower wages and a greater chance of losing their jobs. "It's not surprising that people with these positive attitudes to risk and hierarchy are more likely to work in these small-firm environments before they go off on their own," says Parker. "Small businesses are riskier than large ones, but these people are comfortable with that."

In his research Parker also found that people who start their own firms and subsequently leave them tend to move into the small business sector. This fact further supports the self-selection theory. "There is a very strong sorting back to small firms, and this is a very compelling finding," he says. "There's no reason to expect entrepreneurs to sort at all when they leave entrepreneurship, because their experience is valuable to any firm. But they clearly do."

Another interesting finding is that employees often move to a completely different business sector when they start up their own ventures. Again, this supports self-selection: Less risk-averse individuals are not only more likely to become self-employed, but also more willing to tolerate the uncertainty associated with changing occupations or industries.

Parker was hoping that his study might find greater support for the idea that small businesses played an active role in shaping entrepreneurs. If so, it could argue for new directions in entrepreneurial training or education. "The policy implications of my study are relatively modest," says Parker, "although more entrepreneurship education could perhaps help influence attitudes towards risk."

The evidence that entrepreneurs are self-selecting does have important implications, though, for small and entrepreneurial firms. Many small business owners are concerned that too much autonomy and client access might make employees more likely to leave and start a rival firm. This concern is not borne out by Parker's research. "My results suggest that you needn't worry about training your workers and equipping them with the skills to set up another venture. If small firms are worried about their employees becoming future competitors, they should be more concerned about the risk-taking characteristics of the people they hire."

Parker's study also underlines the importance of a vibrant small business sector. "Small firms have a useful role as place-holders where these budding entrepreneurs often work for a while before making the transition," says Parker. "Although my study does not prove that the transmitting of experience or expertise creates entrepreneurs, my feeling is that the evidence probably understates the productive role of small firms."

In summary, it seems that the ability to deal with risk and uncertainty—important characteristics of any cross-enterprise leader, including entrepreneurs—is sufficient to explain an important phenomenon relating to the origins of entrepreneurship itself. This suggests that cross-enterprise thinking can not only make entrepreneurs more effective, but can also help explain where entrepreneurs come from in the first place.

Conclusion: Entrepreneurship and Cross-Enterprise Leadership

An underlying theme throughout this chapter is that effective entrepreneurs embody the spirit of cross-enterprise leadership.

As the examples discussed in this chapter have shown, entrepreneurs demonstrate many of the important characteristics of cross-enterprise leaders. In addition to being responsible for the operation of the entire business, entrepreneurs face ambiguous situations, uncertain futures and scarce resources with which to address these situations. The environment is often complex and dynamic, typically with an abundance of stakeholders and internal and external networks, resulting in fuzzy organizational boundaries. Yet, despite what seems like insurmountable challenges, many entrepreneurs succeed in building companies that go on to drive growth in the economy. Successful entrepreneurs are able to look at the holistic picture of the enterprise, no matter its size, and see where connections can be made with employees, customers and partners. These kinds of entrepreneurs perhaps can be regarded as the quintessential cross-enterprise leaders.

In this chapter we examined in greater detail some of these links between entrepreneurship and cross-enterprise leadership. We explored the role of mindfulness, creativity and learning to see the benefits that accrue to the entrepreneurs who can develop these characteristics. We also looked at strategizing about customer relations, global expansion via internationalization and R&D networks for competitive advantage. What these examples have demonstrated is that lessons from entrepreneurship also make for good lessons in cross-enterprise leadership, and vice versa. Certainly entrepreneurs have a lot to learn as their businesses grow and become more complex, but the fundamental ideas discussed here illustrate that entrepreneurship has much to offer perspectives on cross-enterprise leadership and the capabilities of cross-enterprise leaders.

~6~

Developing the Cross-Enterprise Leader

BY MARY CROSSAN, JIM HATCH AND GERARD SEIJTS
WITH ASHLEIGH NIMIGAN

What does it take to develop the cross-enterprise leader? Peering into what we do in the classroom provides further insight into the associated challenges and opportunities of developing the cross-enterprise leader outside the classroom. With a strong commitment to teaching excellence, the case study method has been the keystone of Ivey's approach to learning since the school's inception in 1922. Our learning approach has always focused on broad-based, cross-functional, experiential and action-oriented learning. Ivey's case method immerses students in real-world problems that don't fit into tidy functional silos, and as the largest producer of business cases in the world after the Harvard Business School, we are dedicated to constructing learning experiences that place students in challenging contexts that enable them to develop their cross-enterprise leadership capability.

When cross-enterprise leadership was introduced in September 2005, Ivey deepened its investment in leadership development by raising the bar even higher on developing leaders who are better equipped to embrace the challenges and opportunities of the 21st-century leadership context.

Ashleigh Nimigan interviewed three Ivey professors—Mary Crossan (Strategy), Jim Hatch (Finance) and Gerard Seijts (Leadership)—and explored their views on how cross-enterprise leadership has affected their teaching at Ivey, both in substance and style.

Nimigan: *Let's start by clarifying what is meant by cross-enterprise leadership teaching.*

Hatch: What is unique about cross-enterprise teaching is that we take an enterprise-wide approach to the issues being considered as opposed to a narrow concentration on only one functional area of the enterprise. As an example, we may deal with the issue of a merger opportunity. In a traditional finance class the instructor may take a narrow view, such as how to place a value on the acquisition target. Under the cross-enterprise approach many other firm-wide issues would be discussed, including the strategic implications of the merger, the human resources implications and how the company should post-audit the results from the merger. So cross-enterprise teaching broadens the student's perspective of the issue at hand to a total enterprise approach to the problem.

Crossan: Cross-enterprise is not just "cross" within the enterprise but it also captures the view that there is a great deal of economic activity and coordination that happens across a system of enterprises.

As an example, Gerard and I were teaching a case on Campbell Canada, and this organization had to transform its operations to achieve productivity gains by coordinating with its supplier network. Working intimately with suppliers in this way is close to actually making an acquisition of the supplier in terms of the way they're going to have to interface to achieve the productivity gain. So "cross-enterprise" applies both within and across organizations.

Seijts: I would add two things. Jim, you said it well, I think a cross-enterprise leadership case is not just another strategy case and it's not just another leadership case. I think the students should expect anything to happen in a particular case discussion in terms of strategy, finance, accounting, operations, leadership and so forth. So I would say the approach we take in looking at the business problem is holistic—students should be well versed in the various disciplines and be prepared to use a wide range of concepts and management tools in trying to deal with the challenges articulated in the case, such as a merger or a turnaround.

Second, I place an emphasis on leadership in cross-enterprise leadership. In most of the cases we try to get at how you would lead or implement the recommendations. How would you bring meaningful change to the organization? The discussion then proceeds as follows: "Okay, we've identified the issues and offered a set of recommendations, but now how are you going to get traction on your ideas?" And in that discussion, we know the Finance person, the HR person, the Strategy person and so forth have significant insight to add as well.

Hatch: I want to convey that the teaching approach is significantly different at Ivey. We by-and-large don't teach; we create an environment for learning. And that's what's so unique about the case method—we provide students with an opportunity to discuss issues. It's not a one-way transference of material from the instructor to the students who then record it all and repeat it back to us at the end of the term. We provide them with an environment within which they can learn.

And that's very important, because when students graduate from our school, they will continue to engage in lifelong learning. We're not giving them everything they need for life in terms of particular materials and techniques, but we're providing them with an ability to learn on an ongoing basis as they go forward. And we believe that a lot of our classroom environment replicates the kind of learning environment they're going to experience when they get out of here. So they're much more capable of doing that. Ivey is just very different from any other school, and the case method facilitates all of this.

Seijts: I think a good example is the Campbell case. It presents a very messy problem, a highly ambiguous situation. To use an analogy, the case is like a dark room and people are looking for the light switch. The cross-enterprise leadership cases present messy problems, and I know you won't find the answers in a textbook because there's no such thing as a cookie-cutter solution to cross-enterprise challenges. But we force people to think and then to come up with a set of actionable items. Leaders deal with ill-defined problems.

Hatch: As with many MBA programs we do provide tools, techniques and frameworks. But what is challenging about cross-enterprise leadership is that we try to utilize whatever frameworks from whatever functional area that we can to try and solve the problem at hand, and we're quite willing to create new frameworks if necessary to try and solve the problem. That makes Ivey so different.

Nimigan: *So we've touched on it a bit, but what would cross-enterprise leadership teaching look like in a classroom? It would be great if you have an example.*

Crossan: Let me elaborate on the Campbell case we have been speaking about. First of all, it's important to understand why that case was written. It was written as a result of an Ivey Advisory Board Meeting that the faculty had been invited to attend. There was an invited guest speaking about leadership and he asked the faculty if it was resonating with what we do. And we said, "It resonates with what we do and how we think about leadership" but the challenge, to Jim's point, is creating teaching materials for a learning environment, to take what we know about leadership and enable our students to understand what that really feels like. Often, the intimate and critical details lie hidden from view and it may be difficult to bring them to the surface.

David Clark, the former CEO of Campbell, stepped up at that meeting and said, "I can give you the kind of case where you confront difficult and messy issues." We worked on the case together and he has subsequently been in the classroom every time I have taught the case. The students have said that having him there, woven into the case, is critical for their learning. He conducts a role-play in the classroom as if he was the CEO and the students were his management team, to probe how they would deal with these very messy issues.

Our intention is to try and replicate real-world situations that will challenge our students to go beyond cases, textbooks and frameworks. Often lost in management education is the fact that there is an issue to resolve, not just a theory to teach, and furthermore that the issue may not even be apparent. In conjunction with discovering and defining the problem, students are constantly faced with deepening their thinking about cross-enterprise issues and analysis. For example, in the Campbell case, the students were largely focusing on external players when asked about competition. But as it turns out, the biggest competition to Campbell's Canada is actually Campbell's U.S., because they could shut down the Canadian manufacturing in a heartbeat.

So you challenge their thought process to develop an interpretation that is complex, yet gets to the heart of the issue. But that's not where we stop from a learning standpoint; it's not sufficient just to think about it. For example, with the role-play, students have to negotiate with others, begin to develop a collective understanding of what is going on and defend their positions about it—all while having the CEO of the company, who's been through it many, many times before, helping them consider options! Our students learn to think ahead about what it would actually take to implement the kinds of actions that they're suggesting. So they don't think about how an action plan might work in theory, but how they would actually execute their plan.

Seijts: The teaching time can be lengthier in cross-enterprise leadership teaching as well. We often set aside four-hour blocks for one case to allow us to focus in depth on many of the issues that are raised. We try to "call" the students on everything they say or don't say. With the Wal-Mart case, for example, Jim stepped in when Mary was doing her piece and said, "Wait a minute. Are we really enhancing shareholder value?" and another time my colleague in accounting David Sharpe said, "Hold on a second, how can we implement a management control system?" And such moments can occur at any time during the discussion. Sometimes you'll get Fraser Johnson, who gets quite impatient and wants to come to the front of the classroom to refocus the discussion or quiz the students about an Operations detail such as effective management of logistics. So not only should the students be on top of their game, the instructors should be, too!

The four-hour teaching blocks allow us to take extra time to focus on the case and to be a little bit experimental with the people that we invite and the places that we visit. For example, I wrote a cross-enterprise leadership case on the turnaround at the Stratford Shakespeare Festival and in the past we taught the case in Stratford at the Festival Theatre. We also interacted with the Stratford staff including General Director Antoni Cimolino. We also have visited the Walkerton Clean Water Centre to discuss the e-coli outbreak in 2000; seven people died and hundreds became ill after drinking contaminated water. We also did a cross-enterprise leadership session around the start-up of a new organization—Canadian Surgical Technologies and Advanced Robotics. The case was taught at their facilities following a demonstration of a robot in action.

Hatch: Ivey has always had a general management point of view, which essentially means that each person in a functional area has to think more broadly than just the narrow technical material they're dealing with. So in some sense cross-enterprise leadership is not brand new, but rather it builds on strengths that we've had for many years as a school.

When we teach our individual functional courses, probably 75 percent of that class is devoted to functional material and 25 percent will have more of a general management focus where we talk about the implications for the whole organization and other organizations in its space. The case method lends itself to that, because a case typically contains many facts that go far beyond a narrow functional focus. So in a typical functional class, 25 percent of the content might be classified as "cross-enterprise."

In addition to that we have created a number of new cases that are totally devoted to issues that go across the enterprise. In terms of the time devoted to classroom discussion the content may be 25 percent functional and 75 percent cross-enterprise. I wouldn't want to leave the impression that we just periodically bring in cross-enterprise cases and that's the only cross-enterprise experience the students have. The entire program has a focus on cross-enterprise, but its relative emphasis differs depending on which course you're teaching—a functional one or one of these integrated ones.

The examples we've been giving you are truly cross-enterprise. They were designed that way. They have a lot of faculty that are engaged in it and so on. But it's not the only activity we engage in that considers the whole enterprise.

Nimigan: *So how does the case method fit in with cross-enterprise leadership? How do they complement each other?*

Hatch: It's hard to distinguish between those two, because by definition a well-written case has some cross-enterprise component, and it always has if it's a case written by Ivey faculty. Cases used in some schools are simply little problems. They're two pages long and the students are given a modest set of numbers; they have to do a calculation; there is an answer. That is what some schools call "a case." That is not a case at Ivey. A case at Ivey tends to be more complex than that; it draws in broader implications as opposed to just the narrow functional issue at hand. And so virtually every case at Ivey is cross-enterprise in nature. So it's hard, in my mind, to distinguish between the two, except in the way I mentioned already, which is if I'm in a functional field and I have to teach some narrow technical material, that will be much less cross-enterprise than if I've designed a cross-enterprise case to bring out the cross-enterprise implications of things.

Seijts: And typically, when you develop comprehensive cross-enterprise leadership cases they tend to be much longer and harder to write, in part because they need to include perspectives from multiple functional areas.

Hatch: And we devote more classroom time to them. So we're constrained to some extent by the program that says classes are going to be 75 minutes or 80 minutes long. And so you almost have to write shorter cases that are somewhat less complex and somewhat more focused if you have limited class time. Whereas these cross-enterprise cases take place over a four-hour period and we can take many more liberties and bring up many more issues.

Crossan: The kinds of cases we do at Ivey are issue-driven cases. What I see in a lot of so-called cases is history lessons. They contain an interesting story that you need to unpack about what happened in a company, but nobody is put in the position of having to make a decision, to set priorities or to figure out how they would have to implement it. So it's a nice challenge to be able to think about why a company succeeded or failed in something, but it really falls short of where we would want to go with our students. We frequently ask students, "'so what' and what are we going to do about it? What is the issue in here? What's the decision that needs to be made?" Typically the cross-enterprise leadership cases that we have are ones where we highlight one or more issues where a decision or choice has to be made.

Nimigan: *You mentioned cross-enterprise leadership as being about issues. So how do you make sure the students are still developing the tactical skills that they're getting in other MBA programs?*

Seijts: If you start the very first day of the program with complex, messy cases you are likely to lose some students in five minutes or less. There is a need for some basic understanding of balance sheets, value propositions, the principles of leading deep and comprehensive change and so forth. Having said that, we do not let the students off the hook on cross-enterprise leadership even though we are developing functional expertise. There are always opportunities—small or large—to operate in a cross-enterprise leadership manner. One of the cases that comes to my mind is what we do with the General Electric case and the leadership of former CEO Jack Welch. I teach this case early in the program. The students haven't had a strategy class at this point. But I ask my colleagues in Strategy to attend the class. Mary or Michael Rouse can elaborate on some basic strategic choices that are front and center in the case; they can bring greater clarity to the strategy aspect than I possibly can.

Crossan: By focusing strongly on the functional areas of business, as most business schools have done, we may have been doing a disservice to the development of management skills. The problem with business schools focusing solely on the functional fundamentals, in very compartmentalized ways, is that they've done a lot of damage to their graduates because they haven't understood the connectivity to the rest of the organization, to the rest of society and to the industries in which they operate. There has been very narrow functional, myopic thinking in businesses that some may argue has been fueled by business school curricula that have evolved into very narrow functional specialization.

To be flexible and adaptable in the face of uncertainty, my research on improvisation reveals that while you need a fundamental level of expertise, it is not enough. In fact, too great an emphasis on functional expertise may impede creativity and innovation if individuals and organizations do not understand what it takes to move beyond a limited functional focus.

Nimigan: *So we've talked about the differences between the cross-enterprise leadership approach and the traditional approach of other MBA schools. Is there anything else that you want to add about how they're different?*

Seijts: In addition to the cross-enterprise leadership cases throughout our program, we have a specific Cross-Enterprise

Leadership course for MBA students. Unlike many business schools where faculty members are focused on their own course, we are able to work as a team. We have 12 instructors that are involved in teaching the Cross-Enterprise Leadership course; most classes have two or more instructors, sometimes as many as five. I know I can send an e-mail or pick up the phone, and most of the time these individuals are available and willing to help out. You have to have a team orientation in making the classes a success. You need people that are confident working in teams, who are willing to stretch themselves and take an interest in functional areas other than their own, and who step back when it is somebody else's opportunity to lead the class discussion. The instructors need to be flexible and quick thinkers—they should anticipate questions. Instructors challenge one another, thus they better have answers! For example, I can see myself arguing for the necessity of making available the resources for training and development. But Jim might disagree and say, "Look . . . there are more important issues that need to be fixed. How would you justify this expenditure to the Board?" Jim might also ask how we would measure the return on the training interventions. That's a legitimate question.

Hatch: I would say Ivey faculty have a unique set of skills and one of them is that we think outside of our functional areas. There are ways of managing the human resources of business schools. One is to staff the school with technical experts who are stars in very narrow functional areas. They've most likely published a great deal in their area, but they tend to be very narrow in their outlook.

The faculty at Ivey are teacher-scholars in that they need to have expertise in their area of scholarship, which certainly has a functional home, but they possess the desire and capability to excel at embedding that expertise in a broader context. So we all have a functional home and have specific technical expertise, but we're pretty aware of what's going on in other functional areas. It's partly because many of us sit on boards of directors, we consult to companies and we've had business experience; we're not just a narrow group of academics who have gone straight through school studying in a narrow functional area and then gone on to be teachers of that functional area. There is a lot of breadth in our faculty.

And the faculty are specifically chosen for that reason when we hire them. We look at, "Are they team players? Are they flexible? Do they think outside of their functional area? Are they interested in having experience in the real world? Do they interact easily and commonly with business executives?" That's a typical Ivey faculty member.

And although it sounds easy to implement a hiring strategy such as this, it requires an incredible culture, one that Ivey has built up over many years. A business school couldn't simply decide they're going to do what we do tomorrow—it's something that is inbred into our culture. Our culture is the result of careful hiring practices, appropriate incentive systems, a very strong commitment to teaching both individually and in teams, a commitment to the case method, a focus on the practicing manager and support staff that are well trained and flexible in their capabilities. So we have this incredible cultural asset here that is almost uniquely capable of delivering on the cross-enterprise promise.

Crossan: What makes it even more extraordinary is that our culture is counter to what the industry of academia calls for.

Somebody who chooses to come to Ivey is actually going against what is perhaps valued in academia, which is solely research. In academia, individuals increase their mobility as professors by increasing the number of published articles. So why then should somebody care about teaching? Why should they take an interest in anything collaboratively in the organization? Our industry is set up in a way that you are motivated, or should be motivated, to simply publish as much as you can. Professors who come to Ivey are people who actually value teaching in spite of the fact that our industry is not set up to value it. If you value teaching as a professor it means that you're spending a lot of time developing and delivering vibrant courses, that you actually care about being with students and that you care deeply about creating learning experiences that bring the concepts to life. That is a huge investment in time, and it takes away from a faculty's capacity to publish. Although as researchers we love to do research and to publish the results, we are in fact teacher-scholars. Ivey is an institution where people come because they value being a teacher-scholar; they believe that they can do more as a collective than they can do on their own, and so you get a kind of team orientation.

Seijts: While we do a good job, I believe that we still have a ways to go. I think we can do a much better job of putting in place some of the systems or structures that facilitate some of the things that we're trying to do here, like team teaching. In an institution like this, faculty are still being measured on individual performance, but how often do we measure team performance? I think we're making some progress, but I'd like to see a much stronger effort—how can we make team teaching more attractive?

Hatch: A challenge of having many faculty in the classroom at the same time is that it's very costly and requires significant coordination. At some schools, faculty have very clear assigned teaching loads such as teaching two marketing courses in a semester. In most schools, if you were to ask a faculty member to contribute to a course offered jointly with a number of colleagues in return for little recognition and likely no additional pay it could be a problem, even though the outcome could be very beneficial to the institution and the students. There are a number of reasons that this would be a problem.

First, you may find that the faculty would rather teach within the comfort zone of their own discipline. Second, they may want to know, "what is in it for me?" Third, even if the instructor is willing, it is remarkably difficult to get several very busy people to simultaneously find time in their schedules and to meet the schedules of the students. Finally, it is costly to have from two to five well-paid faculty members all in the same room at the same time when they could be doing something else for the organization. Trying to figure out how to manage all of this efficiently and effectively is very difficult to achieve.

The same challenges apply to developing course materials. Having three people write a case is more costly than having one person write a case, especially since all instructors must be aware of each other's approach to the case. It's costly mostly in terms of time but also in terms of the opportunity costs. Again, it would not be easy for a business school to arbitrarily decide they were going to do this when they hadn't been doing this in the past—it's extremely difficult. So there are really big barriers to entry for anybody who wants to be truly cross-enterprise.

If you teach a complex case, it's best if you can do it several times so that you have the economies associated with doing the case. If you're writing a case you have to think of ways to make it less expensive with regards to our time to write that case. And we're continuously improving and experimenting with that. We want to somehow manage that process so it doesn't take too much of everybody's time.

Nimigan: *So why does team teaching work so well with this cross-enterprise leadership approach? What are the benefits of having multiple professors in the same room? Maybe you can talk a bit about how it enhances the student learning experience.*

Seijts: The best feedback I've got in a long, long time was a week or two ago when an MBA student came to me and said, "Gerard, these cross-enterprise leadership cases feel like a workout." The student was mentally tired from what was happening in the classroom. We made him and his fellow students think by asking question after question, and we did not accept superficial answers. He said, "This cross-enterprise approach is the best. This is what business education should be; all of the classes at Ivey should be like this, where you continually stretch people." If you truly engage the students in your class and throw curveballs at them, I think most students get very much excited about the learning process. Cross-enterprise leadership cases facilitate engagement. Earlier I told you I cold-call students in class and they should be able to expect anything.

Although we might have five faculty teaching together in one class, there isn't distraction or chaos. There's a solid teaching plan and a real flow to the discussion. We have an agenda and we plan these things and we get to where we want to be.

Furthermore, students are terribly excited by having multiple faculty in the classroom. It's great value for them! And sometimes they see the faculty disagree and discuss issues among themselves.

I was in a class just the other day, I wasn't teaching actually, I was sitting on the sidelines, but I couldn't help myself . . . I just wanted to get in there as well!

Hatch: All of this partly relates to the case method as well. We believe that in order to learn you have to be engaged. There's a tradition in a lot of business schools that goes something like this: Students read something in a chapter, the professor repeats it in class, maybe doesn't add a huge amount of value to what was in the chapter but maybe explains it a little bit better, they write it down and go home. And so within that kind of a context students can sit back, relax a bit and miss the odd class. Their engagement level is low.

In our classes, the first thing you'll notice is that virtually every student is at every class. It's quite an unusual thing for a student to miss a class, and if they do, you get an e-mail apologizing for missing class. And that's the expectation. So they're here and they know they could be called on at any time, and so they have to be engaged. They can't just sit there and watch because the professor is liable to single them out at any moment and force them to say something and defend themselves in front of their peers. That means they have to be prepared. And so the result is that we have all of the students in class, all of the time, always prepared and always engaged. And you can't imagine how frequently learning environments out there don't provide for this level of engagement.

With a cross-enterprise case you ratchet that engagement up to a higher level because you must come to class prepared to discuss finance for a finance class, but if Gerard is sitting there, you've got to be worried that at any moment he's liable to grab you and take you off into a leadership issue. And so this is the part that blows your mind; you are so incredibly engaged for four hours. When they come out of a class like this they are on a high—the adrenalin is flowing. I've taught at some other schools and most other schools don't achieve that level of engagement.

Seijts: I taught at Toronto and Manitoba prior to joining Ivey. I think that if I met any of those students today, none of them could probably recall any of the lectures I gave. That's actually pretty depressing. I also know that in 10 years from now when I meet Ivey students they will say, "You know, that case or that class is still with me." Of course, that is what you want to happen, to create some memorable learning experiences.

Building on what Jim said, most students want to be engaged. Most students want to be pushed. More and more I get to hear, "You know this course really made me think" or "You were one of the few instructors that didn't accept BS." Sometimes people let a lot of stuff just go by—I try not to. You really have to work for your class contribution grade in my class!

Crossan: The notion that our students have to have a point of view and express themselves is a deep form of learning as we know from all of the research on individual learning. As Karl Weick said, "How do I know what I think until I see what I say?" It is as you express and try to convey to others what is on your mind that you begin to really formulate what is in your head. Otherwise it's very superficial. It's often, "Yes, I get this. We know this." You see this as they try to study for exams—it's in their head. When you ask them to explain it to you they realize, "Well, maybe I don't really get it the way I thought I did."

So this notion of expression goes hand in hand with the case method. It's an incredible learning method that stresses the importance of having a point of view and the ability to express it.

The team-teaching component allows us to attend to cues that are not just about content, but about process. A good example would be from a class that I recently taught. I was observing the broad dynamics of a role-play that was taking place. One faculty member was speaking about something that I knew was fundamental to understanding leadership and organizations, and as I was watching the students take it in I thought, "I'm not sure they understand how profound this is." So I stopped them right there to appreciate that what the professor was talking about is absent in most organizations. In this instance, a point was being made about trust and it was important for the students to understand that they wouldn't be able to execute on any of what had been discussed without understanding what it both takes and means to have the kind of trust amongst the management team.

A key point about process is that while we are developing the content expertise we are actively engaged in developing and promoting the key character elements that support the cross-enterprise leader. Consider elements such as courage, humility and integrity. We seek to deepen a student's understanding and capability for what it takes to be a cross-enterprise leader by activating these character elements in the classroom engagement.

So having several faculty in the classroom allows us to attend to these process issues in ways that is more difficult to do if you're teaching alone. We were trained to do it as faculty members teaching the case method or engaging in case method experience, but it's really delightful having other eyes on the process, and I welcome that when I'm in the classroom with my colleagues.

Seijts: The hands have to go up in the classroom. In many cases all the hands are up, students want to talk. But the best part is when the students disagree with one another, and so once in a while you can let them have a go at one another, and as faculty, we just monitor the debate and pick the best comments and ideas and then we move the discussion forward. In those moments when the students carry the discussion amongst themselves, you know you've touched something.

Nimigan: *How has the case method evolved with cross-enterprise leadership and how is it different?*

Crossan: Cross-enterprise isn't just about having all of these faculty members in the classroom. When we think about the expression of cross-enterprise learning, the learning is embedded in a case and the learning is embedded in the classroom experience. As an example, Jim could be writing a case to use in finance but he might want involvement from Gerard on leadership, and on strategy from me, to make sure he has rounded out the issues. Gerard and I may never teach that case; we may never be in the classroom; but the case that Jim has written has more of a cross-enterprise orientation.

The first few times a case is used we may have five faculty members in the classroom. If I had a marketing colleague in the classroom for the first few runs I can later pick up his or her role and know the kinds of things that they would cover off, having watched them teach it a couple of times. So the learning gets embedded in the faculty as well. That's a really important component of how we get the efficiencies down to where the learning resides with the faculty members and within the case and we bring that full cross-enterprise learning experience to the student in a more efficient manner.

Seijts: It goes back to asking the experts! You said the person might not be involved in teaching the actual case, but I want to make sure I cover the topic in a proper way. What we do is go and talk to the experts to be sure we cover their point of view.

Crossan: A practical example is the Harlequin case, where I had video from my accounting colleague that was used to bring student attention to the issues that he saw and how it related to what they had been covering in accounting. While he wasn't in the classroom, his presence was felt. Of course we had some fun with it and the video started with me approaching him in his office catching him reading a Harlequin romance novel and concluding with him reciting a passage in his eloquent British accent.

Nimigan: *The last question is about the benefits of cross-enterprise leadership.*

Crossan: To answer that question I pose a different question, "Why do we do what we do?" Cross-enterprise leadership requires transformation of the school and of the faculty involved and that transformation is not easy. The answer to why we believe in cross-enterprise leadership stems from examining what leaders need today. I think we are motivated to develop students who can make a difference in the world. We want to equip them with ways of thinking, acting and leading that allow them to make the kind of difference we know will be demanded of leaders. So we're constantly in tune with "what do we think is required, what is amiss?" "Why aren't organizations or leaders able to act and make the kind of difference that we think they can make?" "What is getting in the way?" We're constantly thinking about how it is that we can bring a better learning experience and how to deal with the messy issues, and all of that brings us to cross-enterprise leadership. The capacity to make a difference falls between the functions and organizations and leaders have to have the capacity to figure out how they're going to deal with that kind of complexity and ambiguity. Ultimately, we feel we're equipping our students with the perspectives and approaches that they need to be able to make a difference in the world.

The way many business schools operate today—using the lecture method to develop functional expertise—we find to be very limited. Nice theories and nice approaches, but will it help these students make a difference? We don't think so, and that's why we're investing in cross-enterprise leadership.

Hatch: Sometimes when you talk about leadership, people think that you're taking on the position of the president of the company and that's who the leader is. We do leadership in a much more eclectic way; we believe that you can lead from the bottom. You can be in an entry level job and you can demonstrate leadership.

To illustrate that a little bit: If your boss gave you an assignment, for example, to value a potential acquisition, and as a student you had just been trained to be a technical expert, you could conceivably estimate the value of the target firm. But the challenge is usually more complex than that. It's not only how do you value the company, but should you even acquire it in the first place. Bosses can't always define very clearly what all of the issues are, so what often happens is they give you a fairly narrow task. If you go through your career and just do a whole series of narrow tasks you won't be benefiting that organization in the same way as if you had a perspective of the broad organization, including why this task is being assigned and the additional complexities and issues affecting the task.

We're hopeful that even at an entry level position our students are capable of seeing the bigger picture. When our students get a task, no matter how minor it is, they are able to take the needs of the whole organization into account and they can therefore elevate their contribution to the organization more so than had they limited themselves to the narrow task. We think that perspective will show up in the ability of our students to provide the boss with what he or she really needs rather than just simply delivering on the narrow assignment. And if you continually do that in life, you will get ahead in that organization. You will be recognized and you will be called on, because you're the go-to person that sees the issues, and that is much more helpful.

That's how we view leadership. And that is why we believe in a cross-enterprise approach and why we think it will make a difference to the careers of our graduates.

Crossan: A really neat example given by David Clark during the Campbell case is that leaders and people of influence in the organization see the equivalent of pieces of ice floating on the ocean, and they're everywhere. There are issues everywhere; there are problems to be solved everywhere. The role of leaders is to determine which ones are ice cubes and which ones are icebergs. The ice cubes can be picked off one at a time, compartmentalized, dealt with and put away. The icebergs require a different kind of approach and more attention from a leadership standpoint.

If you're given a problem or an issue, your capacity to see the connectivity to another issue may redefine the problem overall. It may be that the iceberg is the absolute fundamental element in the organization and if we don't pay attention to it, we'll run aground.

Seijts: Another way to look at it is if you have suspects in a line-up, how do you pick out the Ivey MBA grad?

Crossan: The equivalent of that was a question that we got from an MBA prospect during one of our class visitor days. She asked, "If I were at a cocktail party, how would I know who was an Ivey MBA?" Our MBA Director's response was, "This will be somebody who has developed a good capacity to listen, engage others and express a point of view. This is not somebody who sits there passively and lets the world go by. They will be distinguished by their engagement and level of confidence."

Seijts: Confidence, yes. Confidence is a big one. I think we want to prepare the students in the classroom for whatever curveballs people might throw in interviews or assessment center exercises. I have no problem challenging people, they might not always like it, but hopefully at the end of the day they'll develop confidence and recognize that the Ivey classroom was a great "training ground"—a safe place to engage in exchanging ideas to solve messy business problems.

Crossan: It's hard to talk about cross-enterprise divorced from case learning. This notion of confidence is quite important. The process we use in engaging students calls on them to develop some risk muscle about presenting their ideas, often to a large group of people—70 students in the classroom, for example. They learn day in and day out to be able to express themselves in a fashion that's respectful of one another, and learn not to fear criticism. In considering the Ivey MBA some students fear they don't have what it takes to succeed in our classroom. We tell them that all we need is their motivation and willingness to engage. You don't need the capability coming in here. That's our challenge. If you've got the motivation and the will to succeed, then we will work with you to develop the capability to put your ideas out there and not feel personally attacked in the process.

Seijts: I have as a frequent guest speaker in my classroom: businessman and TV host Kevin O'Leary. He discusses several criteria for career success. Number one is communication, the ability to articulate your ideas. Because if you cannot do that, if you're in a leadership position and you're a man or woman of a few words, it's often a disaster. He passionately talks about communication and confidence, and how there is no better place to develop those skills than in our amphitheatre, with 70 other students, and instructors who are really challenging the students. It's great.

* * *

In reflecting on what it takes to develop the cross-enterprise leader in the classroom, there are lessons to be gained for becoming a cross-enterprise leader in the world of business. We have highlighted the importance of having strong technical capability as the table stakes. Having the strategic intelligence, business intelligence, people intelligence and organizational intelligence is critical, but is just not enough. For leaders seeking to elevate their cross-enterprise leadership capability, they need to go beyond these fundamental elements. As Crossan, Gandz and Seijts note in Chapter 3, "Understanding the connection among SI, BI, OI and PI means more than being competent in each area. Having the capacity to anticipate the dynamics of the interrelationships is critical to ensuring that leaders are able to sequence actions in a way that leverages or strengthens a particular area. Every leader and every organization will have strengths and weaknesses in each area. The leadership challenge is to diagnose those strengths and weaknesses to consider the best sequence of actions." As well, they note that the core of cross-enterprise leadership capability is a set of leadership attributes that provides the engine for development of all of the areas. These are the attributes that we develop in the classroom process. In organizations, there are opportunities to develop and deepen them each day, yet the day-to-day firefighting and demand for results may short change and in fact impede the development of these critical attributes.

~7~

Engaging the Chinese Market

BY PAUL W. BEAMISH

Corporate leaders are being rightly pushed by their boards, investors and the media to develop and maintain a coherent international strategy. Such a strategy is intended to incorporate a dominant role for foreign markets in terms of some combination of these countries as markets, sources and/or loci of competition.

Of particular interest in recent years is the role of emerging markets. The largest and fastest-growing emerging market is China. Hence we use it to illustrate how an emerging market might be engaged. The statistics and evidence offered in support of embracing the China market have been overwhelming: China has the largest potential consumer market in the world, is already the second largest economy on a purchasing power parity basis (see column 1 in Exhibit 1), has a growth rate over the past 20 years averaging nearly 10 percent per annum and sees foreign investment in the range of $50 billion per year.

As a consequence, tens of thousands of companies have established some form of operation in or with China, motivated by one or more textbook reasons for venturing into any foreign market. The emphasis on the first of these reasons—sourcing, or resource-seeking—is on securing key supplies or gaining access to factors of production. With China's seemingly infinite supply of low-cost labor, and the way it has been able to commoditize the manufacturing of many goods and processes, entire industrial sectors now source primarily from China on the grounds that it is the only way for them to remain competitive. Such sectors range from electronics to toys.

A second motivation for the focus on China relates to the market itself. China is perceived as an increasingly important market to sell into, particularly as the pace of development quickens. Such a market-seeking orientation allows the investing firm to exploit some inherent skill or competitive advantage it possesses, permitting it to spread its R&D costs over a larger customer base and to provide scale economies.

The third reason why many firms are being exhorted to go to China is because it is the locus of competition. China is where the action is, where firms can scan first-hand what their existing and future competitors are doing, and learn accordingly.

Yet, despite such compelling arguments, thousands of firms have nonetheless opted not to jump on the China bandwagon. They have little, or no, sourcing from China, are not aggressively pursuing Chinese customers and do not have an ear to the ground with regard to new, emerging competitors there. Why? To answer this question, members of the Ivey cross-enterprise research center focused on engaging emerging markets asked

EXHIBIT 1: Emerging Markets: Major Sources of Economic Output

Purchasing Power Parity GDP (Int'l $ Billion) Economic output measured by looking at the prices of a bundle of goods and services at home in local currencies		Gross National Income (GNI) (in US$ Billion) Economic output measured by valuing each country's goods and services in dollars, using three-year average exchange rates		Population (Million)	
USA	14,093	USA	14,574	CHINA	1,325
CHINA	7,909	JAPAN	4,869	INDIA	1,140
JAPAN	4,358	CHINA	3,888	USA	304
INDIA	3,359	GERMANY	3,507	INDONESIA	227
GERMANY	2,905	UNITED KINGDOM	2,827	BRAZIL	192
RUSSIA	2,260	FRANCE	2,696	PAKISTAN	166
UNITED KINGDOM	2,178	ITALY	2,122	BANGLADESH	160
FRANCE	2,122	SPAIN	1,455	NIGERIA	151
BRAZIL	1,978	CANADA	1,454	RUSSIA	142
ITALY	1,872	BRAZIL	1,401	JAPAN	128
MEXICO	1,549	RUSSIA	1,371	MEXICO	106
SPAIN	1,443	INDIA	1,187	PHILIPPINES	90
KOREA	1,344	MEXICO	1,062	VIETNAM	86
CANADA	1,302	KOREA	1,046	GERMANY	82

Source: World Development Indicators database, World Bank, 19 April 2010, for 2008.

Note: Shaded sections signify emerging markets.

dozens of executives working inside and outside China why some companies do not or should not go there. We found that the reasons given by executives for avoiding engagement with the world's largest emerging market were largely chained to an outdated general management paradigm focused on narrow, disaggregated functional disciplines (problems with operations, human resources, marketing and so on). Furthermore, executives tended to invoke narrow rationales for cross-cultural difficulties based on traditional hierarchical command-and-control notions of the firm, rather than viewing their organization and their leadership within it as part of a broader network of value-adding entities with distributed leadership.

Engaging the China market *successfully* requires moving beyond traditional general management approaches to activating a cross-enterprise leadership perspective that is anchored in a deeper strategic commitment to important business issues that permeate functional silos. These business issues include decisions that involve the total enterprise, such as innovation, environmental degradation or health and safety issues. Given the dynamic, complex and uncertain context of emerging markets, traditional general management systems, with their clearly defined functions and organizational boundaries, designed for stable and predictable environments are second-best ways of creating, capturing and distributing value across a network of companies.

Managerial Perceptions of Concerns with the China Market: General Management versus Cross-Enterprise Leadership Approaches

This section details the primary reasons we heard executives give for avoiding engaging with the world's largest emerging market. We demonstrate how, by and large, these reasons reflect a traditional general management perspective to business rather than a cross-enterprise leadership approach, highlighting the missed opportunities along the way. To further illustrate the differences between the two perspectives, we use the research and writing projects undertaken by members of Ivey's Engaging Emerging Markets Centre. We conclude with several recommendations for growing and developing cross-enterprise leaders charged with designing and executing a China strategy.

General Management

Most of the reasons executives provided as to why companies avoid China were anchored in a functional rationale typical of traditional general management models. These arguments can be roughly broken down into problems related to specific departments such as operations, human resources, marketing and legal issues. In what follows, we detail these difficulties as perceived by our panel of executives and described to our research team.

Operations

- **Raw materials and energy shortages** still occur throughout China. It is difficult to maintain manufacturing operations with rotating blackouts or materials shortfalls.

- **Lengthy supply lines** from China are vulnerable to disruption because of port congestion, security-related slowdowns and inadequate infrastructure. As a result, hoped for savings in inventory carrying costs in just-in-time production may be negated by the need to warehouse large quantities of parts due to lengthening supply lines.

Human Resources

- **Employment stability** in China continues to be a significant problem. Workers will literally change jobs for $0.10/hour because even a modest increase of $1.00/day can mean a significant increase in their total annual income. The resultant high employee turnover can have major implications on such areas as quality control, training expense and morale. Some observers have likened it to staffing your factory with a rolling group of summer students. It is hard for North American managers to really appreciate the implications associated with more than 100 million migrant workers in China.

- **The supply of experienced managers** is limited in China. With 127 universities offering MBA and executive MBA programs, China has taken enormous strides to increase the supply of professional managers. This has been supplemented with output from such groups as the National Accounting Institutes, plus Chinese educated abroad who return (known locally as "sea turtles"). Most, however, lack meaningful experience with "best practices" in the west. Those in China with good experience, whether expatriates or locals, are in very high demand. In the absence of an ability to find good quality, affordable management in China, some potential investors prefer to stay home.

- **Employee relations at home** is also an issue that resonates more strongly with some executives than others. The idea of closing down production lines or entire factories, throwing hometown employees into the ranks of the unemployed, is too bitter a pill to swallow for some leaders.

While Japanese-style, life-time employment was never guaranteed, some executives have long felt that they have a moral contract to try to maintain home country employment. To suddenly source product from some real or imagined "sweatshop" in China is not acceptable to them.

Marketing

- **The uneven concentration of target consumers** is a real challenge for many firms marketing in China. The issue is not, of course, one of finding concentrations of people. There are 118 urban districts in China of more than one million people, including 13 with over four million people. The issue is that average wealth levels between these cities vary enormously. Most companies are aware that the citizens of Shanghai have the greatest average income of any city in China, so most companies are marketing in Shanghai. But what about the other provinces and the other urban districts with more than one million people? These districts have per capita annual incomes that are less than half that of Shanghai's. How many widgets or services can you sell if the average citizen is only making $10.00 a day?

- **State-owned enterprises (SOEs) as competitors** in China has given many existing and potential marketers in China real pause. Companies have heard the original horror stories about how China is dominated by SOEs and that some SOEs—which may compete in the same industry—have been allowed to run enormous losses year in and year out. This perception of a lack of normal competitive practices in China, notwithstanding that the central government has been systematically reducing the number of SOEs in the past decade, has meant that some foreign firms have refused to enter the market.

- **Adapting products/services** to the China market is something that some firms are unwilling to do. Such firms have a take it or leave it attitude to Chinese customers. A lack of willingness to adapt to the unique realities of the market—whether in terms of product size, packaging, language or so on—means that most consumers will not purchase. An unwillingness to adapt products or services thus shuts some firms out of the China opportunity.

- **Country of origin** has always been a major issue for international marketers. While a "Made in China" label will not attract any consumer attention when it is on an inexpensive T-shirt at the local Wal-Mart, what if the same label is on a pharmaceutical product, or critical aircraft part? The importance of the country of origin that consumers attach to products varies by industry. In addition, the overall perception of countries as producers of quality products varies as well. China has started in the low-quality, low-cost quadrant and made some progress. However, the experience of other countries suggests that it takes years to achieve dramatic change with regard to country-of-origin effects.

Legal

- **Intellectual property protection** is inadequate or invisible in much of China. Many foreign firms have found to their great discomfort that the processes they have licensed to a Chinese manufacturer have been stolen outright, with no meaningful legal recourse. Creating a low-cost competitor(s) is never the objective of sourcing from China, but sometimes it's the reality.

- **Corrupt practices** in China cause another group of firms to avoid operating there. In emerging nations, where comprehensive legal and regulatory frameworks either do not exist or are not enforced to curtail fraudulent activity, corruption serves to reduce foreign direct investment. Certainly more corruption exists in China than in any of the industrialized countries of the west, according to Transparency International's Corruption Perceptions Index (CPI). No country, of course, has a monopoly on corruption, nor is any country immune from its citizens participating in corruption. Some potential investors simply prefer to delay entering a particular market until overall corruption falls to an "acceptable" level.

- **Import quotas** are being established by a number of foreign governments to stem the impact of cheap Chinese goods, causing some firms to rethink their China exposure. Chinese exports have been so successful in a variety of sectors that different governments have resorted to protectionist practices to protect domestic employment. It is not that there is widespread "dumping" (the sale of goods below the real cost of production). China is simply producing at a lower cost than is observed in other countries. Ironically, the beneficiaries of this use of quotas are some of the emerging markets, such as Bangladesh, Mexico and Brazil, that lost the same jobs to China over the past decade.

- **Legal recourse** is a concern to a number of investors. Does the rule-of-law apply? Is there a level playing field in the event of legal disputes? Some say no.

Cross-Enterprise Leadership

In comparison, rather than focusing on functional constraints as outlined in the previous section, cross-enterprise leaders are able to anchor strategic business decisions, including the go/no go China decision, in important business issues; in complex, uncertain and dynamic environments, there is no such thing as a *manufacturing* issue or a *marketing* issue, there are just *business* issues. Cross-enterprise leaders can see beyond forced departmental silos and consider how important business issues such as innovation can permeate not only across the various units within their own firm, but also across the entire network of value-adding entities with which they interact. For example, many telecommunications companies such as Motorola and Nokia are focused on delivering on innovation and recognize that they must lead across a network of alliances, joint ventures and strategic partnerships to create and capture value in this regard. Both firms have established—not just outsourced—manufacturing facilities in China and have engaged in developing full-scale R&D centers there, including partnerships with researchers at Chinese universities. These arrangements create complex interdependencies that distinguish an "enterprise" from an "organization"; boundaries are less clear and leadership around the core issue of innovation is more distributed throughout the network, rather than dictated in a hierarchical fashion from within a traditional general management paradigm.

Product safety is another business issue that cannot be the responsibility of just one particular functional department. In 2007, Ivey PhD graduate and Engaging Emerging Markets Centre member Dr. Hari Bapuji began exploring the reasons for the many recalls of toy products from China. His analyses (with colleagues at the University of Manitoba) empirically challenged the received wisdom that most of the problems with recalled toys from China were due to mistakes by the Chinese manufacturers. He was able to demonstrate that most recalls were in fact due to design issues, which were the responsibility of the foreign, not Chinese, companies. In fact, the story that unfolds at Mattel in particular is one of a lack of cross-enterprise vision with regard to leadership on the safety issue.

In mid-2007, Mattel faced two different problems: (1) in some toys, excess lead paint and (2) in other toys small magnets that detached and posed an aspiration hazard to children. While the lead paint problem appears to lie within the supply chain and would therefore be typically defined as a manufacturing problem, the small magnet issue is clearly a design flaw and thus more directly Mattel's responsibility. Mattel, however, tried to pin both issues on its Chinese partners invoking an "us versus them" mentality. The failure here, from a cross-enterprise leadership perspective, was to recognize that product safety cannot be an "us versus them" problem, or even a manufacturing versus design issue—safety is inherently a core business issue at the heart of the Mattel enterprise. Leading cross-enterprise means taking an enterprise-wide perspective on core business issues, such as safety or innovation, and making decisions that create and deliver value to all stakeholders.

Exhibit 2 summarizes some of the key differences between a general management and a cross-enterprise leadership approach.

EXHIBIT 2: Differentiating General Management and Cross-Enterprise Leadership

ELEMENT	GENERAL MANAGEMENT	CROSS-ENTERPRISE LEADERSHIP
Entity	• Within organizations • Boundaries defined	• Enterprise – A network of value-adding entities • Boundaries unclear
Context	• Generally stable and predictable • Longer planning horizons	• Complex and uncertain • Dynamic • Real-time
Leadership	• Hierarchial • Managerial focus	• Distributed • Management & leadership focus
Orientation	• Functional anchor	• Issues anchor
Educational approach	• Knowledge	• Think-Act-Lead

Source: Crossan, Mary and Fernando Olivera, 2006, "Cross-Enterprise Leadership: A New Approach for the 21st Century," *Ivey Business Journal Online*, May/June.

The Four Cross-Enterprise Leadership Capabilities and a China Strategy

Other reasons we heard for not engaging the China market related directly to the lack of knowledge, understanding or skills required by a cross-enterprise leader. Crossan and Olivera, as discussed in chapter 1, have described these four cross-enterprise abilities as strategic, business, people and organizational intelligence. The first of these, strategic intelligence, requires a fundamental understanding of the business context—an ability to see opportunities and threats before they arise as well as an ability to focus beyond the short-term dictates of share price to the longer-term implications of strategic decisions. To illustrate, we found that complacency is at the root of why another group of firms said they have not gone to China. The leaders of these firms are comfortable with the status quo and are either unable or unwilling to embrace change. These executives maintain an attitude that "China" is one more fad of the day that will not affect them, or that its impact will be negligible. Similarly, ethnocentrism still exists in many organizations in industrialized countries. There is a belief in some circles that there is nothing to be learned about best practice as a consequence of doing business in China. Worse, no value is attached to seeing, first-hand, the creation of future China-headquartered competitors. It doesn't matter that China already has 37 of its companies among the Fortune Global 500 largest firms. Despite this fact, some foreigners refuse to believe it could happen. Lastly, some executives focused on the fact that service sector jobs have not migrated in great numbers to China. Unlike India, with its English-speaking, more IT-savvy population, no large-scale, externally focused comparable service sector has emerged in China—yet. However, some service sector executives simply could not see this strategic opportunity, demonstrating a deficit in the type of "strategic intelligence" required for cross-enterprise leadership.

The second type of intelligence is business intelligence, which relates to understanding the fundamental nuts and bolts of the business you're in. Many of the leaders we talked to about going into China may have lacked this business intelligence because of the age of their firm. Acquiring all of the knowledge that one needs (including the portfolio of traditional general management skills like marketing, finance, operations and so on) takes time—and understanding how these connect across departments, units, businesses, alliances, partnerships and networks takes even more time. In international management, this difficulty is known as *the liability of age*—in practice, newly established enterprises simply are unlikely to either source immediately from China or market immediately to China. While there are many examples of so-called "born global" organizations, these nonetheless are more the exception than the rule. While Research In Motion might immediately view "the world" as its target market, a new furniture manufacturer would initially have a much more local or, at best, national orientation. Young organizations initially suffer high failure rates. Young organizations that need to also understand a complex foreign market such as China face an even greater hurdle. Similarly, *the liability of foreignness* suggests that when firms are first expanding abroad, they tend to focus on markets that are geographically close, and where language and cultural differences seem surmountable. For many North American or European leaders, China is indeed "foreign," in fact "too foreign" for some firms to try and source from. These firms may lack leaders with sufficient business intelligence to engage in a China strategy.

Organizational intelligence, the third type of intelligence required for cross-enterprise leadership, requires a solid command of the firm's structures, procedures and compensation systems that drive the culture of the organization. In many respects, the majority of the comments we heard for avoiding China—from operational difficulties to legal barriers—suggest organizational cultures that are resistant to change (complacent, ethnocentric, unwilling to adapt). The *liability of size* is another example of how leaders of small firms in particular might lack the kind of organizational intelligence required to move forward with a China strategy. With all the attendant resource constraints that small organizations face, sourcing directly from China or marketing directly to China might not be among the first steps taken by most small organizations. Since many of the steps required to source from China or market to China are going to be the same for small or large firms, the small firm might not have the sales volume to spread the financial risk of the effort across.

Lastly, cross-enterprise leaders must have people intelligence. In a complex, uncertain and dynamic market such as China, the ability to listen, understand, motivate and inspire organizational members is even more challenging. However, without people intelligence, the effectiveness of certain leaders will be greatly curtailed. In China, this manifests itself specifically as *the liability of relational orientation,* speaking to the heavy use of joint ventures. While it is possible to have a purely contractual sourcing arrangement from China, for example, leaders that take an arms-length approach with suppliers are often met with unpleasant delays and surprises. As a consequence, many investors choose to form joint ventures in China, even though the regulations today do not require it. These investors want a partner who can provide knowledge of the local economy, politics and culture. Yet some potential investors do not like joint ventures and do not like partners. They prefer to do it themselves, or not at all. Those with a do-it-themselves rather than relational orientation may not be willing to invest in developing the social and political connections required—in other words, the people intelligence needed to lead cross-enterprise. This is so very different from China, a country with a long tradition of *guanxi*—a system of personal contacts, networks and relationships.

As we've mentioned, in conjunction with general intellect, these four "intelligences" are the basic ingredients of cross-enterprise leadership capability—a leadership approach that is well suited for engaging emerging markets.

The research on toy recalls from China led to a series of practical recommendations in regard to ways in which a company could reduce its design flaws. These recommendations, essentially, call for building up the stores of strategic, business, organizational and people intelligence required for leading on the product safety issue (see Exhibit 3).

EXHIBIT 3: Steps Companies Can Take to Reduce Design Flaws

First, firms should establish a learning culture in which employees feel safe reporting their concerns about design flaws and in which mistakes are not ignored. Such a culture begins with managers being receptive to employees' ideas and criticisms. Companies should also engage in *reactive* learning: Once a product flaw is discovered, the firm should examine and improve the systems and processes that contributed to it. In addition, companies should engage in the four major types of *proactive* learning:

Study, Listen, Test, Track.

Study competitors' recalls, overall recall trends, issues leading to recalls, regulators' comments, and even medical journals, which sometimes report health problems resulting from product use or misuse.

Listen to design and test engineers, whose concerns are often downplayed or overlooked in the excitement of taking a new product to market.

Test effectively for safety issues. Too many toy companies rely on live humans to test product appeal but not safety features. While dummies are clearly appropriate in crash-testing carseats and the like, many companies can spot potential dangers by having people use products in realistic settings. At the least, such tests would guide companies in providing clearer instructions and warnings.

Track customer feedback to look for patterns that might reveal product flaws.

Doing all this properly requires that companies buck the trend of downsizing design and testing departments. It also requires that teams be set up to monitor the vast amount of useful information out there, from recall data to customer complaints. And it requires that these teams be coordinated at the highest organizational level—by the executives with responsibility for looking, unflinchingly, at the big picture.

Source: Bapuji, Hari and Paul W. Beamish, 2008, "Avoid Hazardous Design Flaws," *Harvard Business Review*, 86(3): 23, 26.

Engaging Emerging Markets—Cross-Enterprise Leadership Centre

The research into toy recalls from China illustrates one of the most important roles for any business school—the generation of intellectual capital or the continuous development of new insights and new models for the discovery of best practices that have direct relevance to managers today. Schools that deliver cutting-edge research not only provide real value to the academic community but also ensure that their programs are consistently renewed with new insights, which have a direct effect on the business community. At Ivey, the Engaging Emerging Markets Cross-Enterprise Leadership Centre is dedicated to research that helps executives overcome some of the perceived barriers listed in this chapter and to pursue the myriad of opportunities that lie within the borders not only of China but other emerging markets as well.

Exhibit 4 provides a more detailed framework for the ongoing research on engaging emerging markets at Ivey. It contains examples of the types of issues and phenomena that Centre members have pursued or are currently investigating. Many other issues undoubtedly will be pursued in the future.

EXHIBIT 4

Examples of Research on Engaging Emerging Markets

Entering Emerging Markets

Operating in Emerging Markets

- Internationalization
- IPP
- Country Selection
- Industry Analysis
- Entry Mode
- Sourcing
- Partner Selection

- Culture Shock
- Ethical Dilemmas
- Negotiations
- Transferability of Business Models
- Political Risk

- Asymmetric Expectations
- (Alliance) Reorganizations
- Market Exit
- Managing in Economic Crisis Environments
- Effects of Market Reforms

- Developing a "China" Strategy
- EM2EM Trade/Investment

- Trade with Emerging Market Firms
- FDI from Emerging Market Firms

Engaging Emerging Market Competitors

Some of the other research initiatives that Centre members have undertaken include tracking the evolving nature of the Chinese market, exploring the emerging market to emerging market (EM2EM) opportunity and partnering with emerging market enterprises to generate teaching cases. Each of these projects is designed to respond to the perceptions of managers about why they might wish to avoid China.

For example, Ivey PhD graduate and Centre member Dr. Andrew Delios (now at National University of Singapore) has been exploring the many transformations underway in China,[1] including developments in the manufacturing sector. Many of the very low-cost manufacturers that originally sprouted among China's coastal cities first moved to less expensive inland cities years ago. However, even these inland locations are now too expensive as manufacturing locales, and, as a result, some of these low-cost manufacturers are now leaving China altogether. One of the realities of the Chinese market is the very rapid speed of change. In the west, economic growth of 2 percent per year would be celebrated, but in China this is typical of quarterly growth. If the market is growing four times as fast (or faster) in China as it is in North America or Western Europe, and as a leader you haven't visited China in a few years, your understanding of current market reality could be the western equivalent of a decade out of date! Good leaders are reassessing very frequently the rules of thumb they have developed about how markets such as China actually work.

Similarly, some business leaders might feel that the business taking place between emerging markets is not relevant to their organization. However, they would be wrong. When, for example, firms from two major emerging markets join forces

1 Delios, A. and X. Ma, 2010, "China Is Undergoing a Transformation... Yet Again," *Ivey Business Journal Online*, January/February; Delios, A., P.W. Beamish and Z. Xuejuan, 2009, "The Evolution of Japanese Investment in China," *Asia-Pacific Business Review*, 15(3): 323–345.

to compete internationally, they can represent a formidable competitor for a North American– or European–based firm. Ivey marketing professor and Centre member Dr. Niraj Dawar has long been interested in the realities of EM2EM trade. Among many observations, Dr. Dawar has recently highlighted the need for multi-national enterprise leaders to define their strategic stance relative to "this EM2EM awakening" and to shed overhead costs in their organizations to gain competitiveness.

Lastly, in addition to the three aforementioned illustrative examples of how research can better inform the perceptions of business leaders, field-based case writing also can play a major role. Exhibit 5, beginning on page 142, provides short abstracts for dozens of available case studies about entering China, doing business in China and engaging Chinese competitors, in which the benefits of a cross-enterprise leadership approach can be found.

Conclusion

The development of a China strategy, let alone a strategy for all emerging markets, is a major challenge for any leader—in fact, the list of challenges may occasionally seem to be insurmountable. However, many of the reasons we heard for avoiding doing business with China were anchored in old-fashioned functional "silo-thinking," rather than focused on how thinking cross-enterprise might help firms successfully tackle core business issues. Business firm leaders are called upon increasingly to deal with the complexity of a rapidly changing and uncertain context. Firm boundaries are becoming less distinct and traditional command and control hierarchical systems simply are not flexible enough to truly leverage the value within complex networks of alliances and partnerships. A genuinely cross-enterprise leadership approach is necessary.

Luckily, strategic, business, organizational and people intelligence can be learned. The first step in developing strategic intelligence with regard to a China strategy is to simply get out from behind the desk and go to China to begin to reduce the uncertainty around the go/no go decision and to fully assess the risk/return trade-offs. This includes seeing beyond traditional barriers to strategic opportunities not just for the immediate short term, but for the longer-term horizon as well. Business intelligence can be honed through further training and development or job rotation programs that stretch leaders out of their comfortable areas of expertise. This cross-exposure can help leaders understand the important links across functional areas and leverage important knowledge regarding key strategic issues throughout the organization and the broader enterprise as well.

Organizational intelligence requires a candid examination of the structures, systems, procedures and policies within the firm that might be contributing to an organizational culture resistant to a China strategy, while developing people intelligence is anchored in a commitment to listen, learn, understand and motivate individuals to achieve extraordinary results. All four intelligences, as well as a certain degree of general intellect, are the basic ingredients of cross-enterprise leadership capability. The leadership challenge for those executives tasked with developing and executing a China strategy is to honestly diagnose their strengths and weaknesses in each area and commit to developing the skills required to lead cross-enterprise.

At the Engaging Emerging Markets Research Centre at Ivey, our objective is to conduct well-executed research in this area. By studying important issues, we hope to be in a position to better inform not only those cross-enterprise leaders charged with developing a China strategy, but also to assist any organization as they engage the world's other emerging markets.

EXHIBIT 5: Case Studies about Entering China, Operating in China, and Engaging Chinese Competitors

Entering China

NES China: Business Ethics (A) [9B01C029]
Joerg Dietz, Xin Zhang

NES is one of Germany's largest industrial manufacturing groups. The company wants to set up a holding company to facilitate its manufacturing activities in China. They have authorized representatives in their Beijing office to draw up the holding company application and to negotiate with the Chinese government for terms of this agreement. In order to maximize their chances of having their application accepted, the NES team in Beijing hires a government affairs coordinator who is a native Chinese and whose professional background has familiarized her with Chinese ways of doing business. NES's government affairs coordinator finds herself in a difficult position when she proposes that gifts should be given to government officials in order to establish a working relationship that will better NES's chance of having its application approved. This method of doing business is quite common in China. The other members of the NES team are shocked at what would be considered bribery and a criminal offence in their country. The coordinator must find a practical way to bridge the gap between working within accepted business practices in China and respecting her employers' code of business ethics. The (B) case (9B01C030) gives a brief summary of the eventual solution to this problem.

Sun Life Financial: Entering China [9B04M066]
Paul W. Beamish, Ken Mark, Jordan Mitchell

Sun Life Financial is a large insurance conglomerate with $14.7 billion in annual revenues. The vice-president for China must formulate an approach for his company's entrance into China. Sun Life has achieved two important milestones: the right to apply for license and the signing of a Memorandum of Understanding for Joint Venture with China Everbright, a local securities company. The financial vice-president must consider strategic options for entry and choose a city in which to focus his efforts in getting a license. In doing so, he needs to consider Sun Life's overall priorities, strategic direction and how he will sell the concept to senior management in Canada. Intended for use in an introduction to international business course, the case includes assessing internal capabilities against an environmental scan, formulating strategy and making operational decisions relating to city selection. It also introduces the idea of joint venture management and government relations.

Palliser Furniture Ltd.: The China Question [9B04M005]
Paul W. Beamish, Jing'an Tang

Palliser is Canada's second largest furniture company. The company has production facilities in Canada, Mexico and Indonesia and experimented with cutting and sewing leather in China. The company is looking at further expanding the relationship with China. Ever since Palliser set up a plant in Mexico, the company has faced increasing competitive pressure from Asia, especially from China. The president of Palliser must decide what form this relationship should follow: Should it be an investment, either wholly or partly owned, or should it be through subcontracting?

Majestica Hotel in Shanghai? [9B05M035]
Paul W. Beamish, Jane Lu

Majestica Hotels Inc., a leading European operator of luxury hotels, was trying to reach an agreement with Commercial Properties of Shanghai regarding the management contract for a new hotel in Shanghai. A series of issues require resolution for the deal to proceed, including length of contract term, name, staffing and many other control issues. Majestica was reluctant to make further concessions for fear that doing so might jeopardize its service culture, arguably the key success factor in this industry. At issue was whether Majestica should adopt a contingency approach and relax its operating philosophy, or stick to its principles, even if it meant not entering a lucrative market.

PepsiCo Changchun Joint Venture: Capital Expenditure Analysis [9B00N016]
Larry Wynant, Claude P. Lanfranconi, Peter Yuan, Geoff Crum

PepsiCo Inc. spanned more than 190 countries and accounted for approximately one-quarter of the world's soft drinks. The vice-president of finance for PepsiCo East Asia had been collecting data on the firm's proposed equity joint venture in Changchun, China. While PepsiCo was already involved in seven joint ventures in China, this proposal would be one of the first two green-field equity joint ventures with PepsiCo control over both the board and day-to-day management. Every investment project at PepsiCo had to go through a systematic evaluation process that involved using capital budgeting tools such as new present value and internal rate of return. The vice-president needed to decide if the proposed Changchun joint venture would meet PepsiCo's required return on investment. He also was concerned what the local partners would think of the project. The final decision would be made after a presentation to the president of PepsiCo Asia-Pacific.

Beijing Toronto International Hospital [9B01A006]
Kenneth G. Hardy, Ken Mark

Beijing Toronto International Hospital was a new private facility being built in Beijing that would offer a full range of general and specialized Western-quality medical services to a very specific market segment: expatriates and wealthy Chinese families. Membership cards were sold that entitled each member to a distinct level of hospital service. The chief executive officer found that as the building neared completion, only a few memberships had been sold, which resulted in a cash shortage. He did not know why sales failed to materialize as expected, but felt that he must redirect and revitalize the marketing campaign. He considered several options and had to determine what would work best in the Chinese market.

Textron Ltd. [9B01M070]
Lawrence Beer

Textron Ltd. is a family-owned manufacturer of cotton- and sponge-fabricated items. The company wants to expand its business with an offshore manufacturing enterprise that will fit with the company's policy of caring for their employees and providing quality products. The company is looking at two options: a guaranteed outsourcing purchase agreement or a joint venture. After several meetings with offshore alliance candidates the vice-president of the company must analyze the cross-cultural differences to established corporate guidelines of global ethics and social responsibility that the company can use in their negotiations with a foreign manufacturing firm.

Scotts Miracle-Gro: The Spreader Sourcing Decision [9B08M078]

John Gray, Michael Leiblein, Shyam Karunakaran

The Scotts Miracle-Gro company is the world's largest marketer of branded consumer lawn and garden products. Headquartered in Marysville, Ohio, the company is a market leader in a number of consumer lawn and garden and professional horticultural products. The case describes a series of decisions regarding the ownership and organization of the assets used to manufacture fertilizer spreaders. This case is intended to illustrate the application of and trade-offs between financial, strategic and operations perspectives in a relatively straightforward manufacturing "make-buy" decision. The case involves a well-known, easily described product that most students would assume is made overseas. Sufficient information is provided to roughly estimate the direct financial cost associated with internal (domestic) production, offshored (non-domestic) production and outsourced production. In addition, information is included that may be used to estimate potential transaction costs as well as costs associated with foreign exchange risk.

Operating in China

Nike Inc.: Developing an Effective Public Relations Strategy [9A99C034]

Kathleen E. Slaughter, Donna Everatt

In the early 1990s, the first article surfaced alleging that factories subcontracted by Nike in China and Indonesia were forcing workers to work long hours for low pay, and for physically and verbally abusive managers. The article was the seed of a media campaign that created a public relations nightmare for the company. A financial crisis in Asia and intense competition in the domestic market contributed to a decline in Nike's revenue and market share after three years of record performance. Though no direct correlation could be proven between the consumer's negative perceptions of Nike and the company's decline in market share and stock, it certainly did not help in their efforts to establish themselves as the global leader in a hotly competitive industry. A linear overview of the adverse publicity that Nike received, and the perspectives of Nike senior management, demonstrates to students the importance and elements of the timely development of an effective media and consumer relations campaign.

Taming the Dragon: Cummins in China (Condensed) *[9B05M034]*

Charles Dhanaraj, Maria Morgan, Jing Li, Paul W. Beamish

This case documents more than 15 years of U.S.-based Cummins, a global leader in diesel and allied technology, and its investment activities in China. While the macro-level indicators seem to suggest the possibility to hit $1 billion in revenues in China by 2005, there were several pressing problems that put into question Cummins' ability to realize this target. Students are presented with four specific situations and must develop an appropriate action plan. They are related to the respective streamlining and consolidation of several existing joint ventures, distribution and service, and staffing. The case presents the complexity of managing country-level operations and the role of executive leadership of a country manager.

Great Wall Golf & Country Club [9B00M003]
Paul W. Beamish, Donna Everatt

The newly hired director of human resources for a large golf and country club near Beijing, China, has just presented her human resources plan to the company's founder. At issue is whether this plan—in terms of recruiting, training and development, rewards and benefits—was directionally correct and implementable.

Bax Global Limited: Staff Turnover in Mainland China [9B05C035]
Jean-Louis Schaan, Nigel Goodwin

The human resources manager for logistics and supply chain management at BAX China must consider her company's high rate of staff turnover: 12 percent in the first eight months of the year. She must evaluate the company's current methods of dealing with turnover and consider what additional action should be taken. The case offers a uniquely Chinese perspective on workforce recruitment, management and retention. Logistics was a complex and rapidly growing industry in mainland China. Many multinational and domestic service providers were entering the market and expanding their operations; however, these companies had to respond to complex operational challenges and escalating customer demands. The resulting demand for skilled workers led to high turnover rates across the industry and at all organizational levels, and created margin pressure and other management challenges. The industry and the broader economy were growing rapidly. Skilled workers were in short supply because logistics was a new and developing discipline. Also, in the human resources manager's opinion, cultural attitudes resulted in low loyalty among the workers.

Mattel and the Toy Recalls (A) [9B08M010]
Hari Bapuji, Paul W. Beamish

On July 30, 2007, the senior executive team of Mattel, under the leadership of Chief Executive Officer Bob Eckert, received reports that the surface paint on Sarge Cars, made in China, contained lead in excess of U.S. federal regulations. It was certainly not good news for Mattel, which was about to recall 967,000 other Chinese-made children's character toys because of excess lead in the paint. The decision ahead was not only about whether to recall the Sarge Cars and other toys that might be unsafe, but also how to deal with the recall situation. The case details the events leading up to the recall and highlights the difficulties a multinational enterprise faces in managing global operations.

Mattel and the Toy Recalls (B) [9B08M011]
Hari Bapuji, Paul W. Beamish

On August 14, 2007, the U.S. Consumer Product Safety Commission, in cooperation with Mattel, announced five different recalls of Mattel's toys. On September 4, Mattel announced three more recalls. Some were due to the use of lead paint, while others were due to small magnets coming loose. The case outlines the handling of the recalls and their consequences, such as consumer outrage, media scrutiny, government intervention and the effect on China. Further, it discusses the design flaws for which large toy companies are responsible. The case raises issues such as who Mattel's stakeholders are, what values Mattel followed and whether Mattel needs to revisit its China strategy.

Spin Master Toys (A): Finding a Manufacturer for E-Chargers [9B01D001]
John S. Haywood-Farmer, Ken Mark

Spin Master Toys was a Canadian manufacturer of toys ready to produce its latest product, E-Charger, an electrically powered model airplane. The operations manager had to decide which supplier should design and manufacture this new product. The time frame from design to delivery was very short, requiring an accelerated development schedule. The company had a short-list of two potential companies, both located in the major toy manufacturing district of southern China, near Hong Kong. The operations manager had to develop the appropriate criteria for this decision and evaluate the two suppliers. With relatively little information and already behind schedule, the company must make its decision in the face of considerable uncertainty. The supplemental (B) & (C) cases follow the progress and the challenges of the production of the E-Charger.

Worldwide Equipment (China) Ltd.: A Sales Performance Dilemma [9B02A028]
June Cotte, Alan (Wenchu) Yang

Worldwide Equipment Ltd. is one of the world's largest manufacturers of heating, ventilating and air conditioning equipment. The Beijing regional sales manager has just heard that the sales performance of his office ranked the lowest among the sales offices in China. The Beijing sales force will not receive their year-end bonus unless the situation can be turned around quickly. He must determine whether the sales management process or a recent new hire on the sales force, whose hiring was strongly suggested by the manager's boss, are to blame for the poor sales performance, and how to keep the situation from recurring.

Wuhan Erie Polymers Joint Venture [9B03C002]
Thomas Begley, Cynthia Lee, Kenneth Law

The Erie Performance Polymers division manager in China and general manager of Wuhan Erie Polymers joint venture has just received approval for his requested transfer to divisional headquarters in the United States. In preparation, a key decision concerns his successor. He has received information on six candidates under consideration and knows that his recommendation will carry heavy weight in the final decision. The general manager has attempted to inculcate in his mainly Chinese workforce an appreciation for Western business practices and an ability to enact them. At the same time, acknowledging their substantial differences, he has tried to mix elements of both Chinese and Western values in creating a culture for the joint venture. He believes strongly that his successor must be responsive to the tensions between the relevant cultures. As he compares them, he wonders which candidate has the best set of qualities to succeed him as general manager.

Carrefour China, Building a Greener Store [9B08M048]
Andreas Schotter, Paul W. Beamish, Robert Klassen

Carrefour, the second largest retailer in the world, had just announced that it would open its first "Green Store" in Beijing, before the 2008 Olympic Games. David Monaco, asset and construction director of Carrefour China, had little experience with green building and was struggling with how to translate that announcement into specifications for store design and operations. Monaco had to evaluate the situation carefully both from ecological and economic perspectives. In addition, he had to take the regulatory and infrastructure situation in China into account, where no official green building standard exists and only a few suppliers of energy-saving equipment operate. He already had collected energy and cost data from several suppliers and wondered how this could be used to decide among environmental technology options. Given that at least 150 additional company stores were scheduled for opening or renovation during the next three years in China, the project would have long-term implications for Carrefour.

Engaging Chinese Competitors

Yunnan Baiyao: Traditional Medicine Meets Product/ Market Diversification [9B06M088]
Paul W. Beamish, George Peng

In 2003, 3M initiated contact with Yunnan Baiyao Group Co., Ltd. to discuss potential cooperation opportunities in the area of transdermal pharmaceutical products. Yunnan Baiyao (YB) was a household brand in China for its unique traditional herbal medicines. In recent years, the company had been engaged in a series of corporate reforms and product/market diversification strategies to respond to the change in the Chinese pharmaceutical industry and competition at a global level. By 2003, YB was already a vertically integrated, product-diversified group company with an ambition to become an international player. The proposed cooperation with 3M was attractive to YB, not only as an opportunity for domestic product diversification, but also for international diversification. YB had been attempting to internationalize its products and an overseas department had been established in 2002 specifically for this purpose. On the other hand, YB also had been considering another option, namely whether to extend its brand to toothpaste and other healthcare products. YB had to make decisions about which of the two options to pursue and whether it was feasible to pursue both.

Cola Wars in China: The Future Is Here [9B03A006]
Niraj Dawar, Nancy Dai

The Wahaha Hangzhou Group Co. Ltd. is one of China's largest soft-drink producers. One of the company's products, Future Cola, was launched a few years ago to compete with Coca-Cola and PepsiCo and has made significant progress in the soft-drink markets that were developed by these cola giants. The issue now is to maintain the momentum of growth in the face of major competition from the giant multinationals and to achieve its goal of dominant market share.

Midea: Globalization Challenge for a Leading Chinese Home Appliance Manufacturer [9B00A031]
Niraj Dawar, Peter Yuan

The managing director and director of overseas marketing of Midea Group, China's largest air conditioner manufacturer, had concerns about the company's domestic and global competitive position. They felt the company needed to develop a strategy to defend its home market in the wake of more liberalized imports and simultaneously develop the resources and skills required to play in a global market where its cost advantages had been nullified because international players also were exporting from China. To do so, they needed to review the company's current international strategy and examine both branding and private label options.

China Kelon Group (A): Diversify or Not? [9B03M004]
Paul W. Beamish, Justin Tan

In 1998 the soon-to-retire founder of China Kelon Group, a major home electrical appliance manufacturer, was confronting issues of market diversification (urban to rural), product diversification (refrigerator manufacturer now also producing air conditioners), and the evolution of his senior management team (from an entrepreneurial firm to one managed by professional managers). Besides offering a context to address the above issues, this case illustrates to a non-Chinese audience just how rapidly local Chinese manufacturing has developed and that such firms are future competitors for foreign companies. It also helps students explore the broader question about the ability of founder/entrepreneurs to effectively manage the transition to becoming a larger, more diversified company. Supplement to this case is China Kelon Group (B): Integration After Merger, product number 9B03M005.

Gome—King of China's Electrical Appliance Retail Chain [9B06M098]
Shigefumi Makino, Anthony Fong

The chairman of Gome Ltd., a well-known appliance retail chain, congratulated his management team for their excellent performance over the past year. For three consecutive years, Gome had been ranked the largest electrical appliance retail chain in China, and the second largest overall retail chain. Claiming to be the only true national player, Gome achieved total sales of RMB23.9 billion in 2004 and in 2005 doubled its number of stores to 426. The company's four-year plan is to capture 10 to 15 percent of the market share nationally. Gome would need to double the number of stores in the coming three years, and more importantly, it would need to work out a strategy to fend off its local and global competitors.

China Minmetals Corporation and Noranda Inc.
[9B06M013]
Isaiah A. Litvak

The proposed takeover of Noranda Inc. (one of the biggest mineral players in the world) by the Chinese state-owned enterprise China Minmetals Corporation was cause for Canadian government concern as it required some understanding about the workings and objectives of state-owned enterprises. There was particular concern around the labor issues and human rights violations in China, and the possible impact of these on the proposed takeover. Equally important, Canada ran the substantial risk of sending the wrong message to China if it was to block such a takeover, and in some respects, to be seen as shutting its doors to one of the world's largest and most powerful emerging economies.

~8~

Greed Is Never Good: Cross-Enterprise Leadership and the Social Responsibilities of Business

BY JEFFREY GANDZ

In the wake of the financial meltdown and global economic recession of 2007–2009, there has been a very sharp rise in global condemnation of business and a real questioning of the capitalist system, at least as it is unfolding in the United States, the U.K. and other "advanced" economies. Whether deserved or not, it is clear that this criticism is prompting a reconsideration of the social responsibility of business leaders. More and more of them are recognizing it is simply not good sense to make a mess in their own backyards. Moreover, if they make their own backyards great places to live and work, and if they make obvious contributions to important issues such as reducing climate change, feeding the poor or other social issues, this may draw customers, employees and investors to the corporation.

While caring for society is a noble and worthy virtue in and of itself, it is also an act of enlightened self-interest. This view differs from "greed" in that it recognizes self-interest and the interests of others in society and seeks to maximize self-interest subject to the consequences for others. Its moral foundation rests on recognizing, integrating or balancing legitimate interests, whereas greed is the pursuit of self-interest in ignorance of, or despite, the interests or needs of others. The central thesis of this chapter is that this perspective must be embraced by anyone who sees themselves as a cross-enterprise leader since the societal impact of any significant decision made by any leader redounds to the benefit or harm of the corporation.

In the shadows of the recent financial meltdown and global recession, an old debate has been rekindled: Should corporate managers be required to be socially responsible, or should they confine themselves solely to pursuing shareholder value by all legal means? This debate is taking place in capitalist economies in which deregulation of financial markets has been going on for at least 20 years, economies in which many government officials mistakenly believe that "the marketplace" will govern enterprise behaviors in the interest of society.

The financial and economic crises of 2007–2009 provided a good deal of ammunition to those who doubt the viability of the capitalist system as we have experienced it through the last 50 years. It is a system that has generated great wealth, albeit unevenly distributed, raised the standard of living of millions of people around the world and been embraced in one form or another by emerging economies. In recent years, however, it has been severely tested and found wanting.

Capitalism has always had its detractors. There were those who inveighed against the moneylenders in the temple in biblical days, struggled against feudalism, and railed against class-based dominance and the exercise of power based on economic ownership in the last century. Today the attacks continue despite, or perhaps because of, the pervasive and growing presence of corporations on the arts and cultural scenes, in amateur and professional sports, social services, education and many other facets of society.

In modern times, the debate has been less about whether capitalism is good or bad and more about the extent to which business enterprises should be controlled and regulated by the state for the overall good of society. Most recently, lawmakers in the United States, the United Kingdom and several countries within the eurozone have gone so far as to suggest that the creation of, and trading in, complex derivatives, synthetic collateralized debt obligations and other structured products should be prohibited on the grounds that they are highly leveraged products that threaten the stability of national and global economies.

No one would deny the ultimate right of governments to limit commercial activity in the interests of the common good. However, many of the critics of firms such as Goldman Sachs, AIG, JPMorgan Chase and others have suggested that these companies were socially irresponsible for ever having developed and marketed these products and should have restrained themselves from doing so even though laws and regulations permitted it.

What do cross-enterprise leaders need to know about this relationship between business and society? What are the issues? What's at stake? What should be their roles in a world that seems to be demanding more of its corporate leaders than just the pursuit of shareholder returns?

A Historical Perspective

The modern debate about the role of business owners and managers in society took shape in the 1930s. The economic bubble of the Roaring Twenties had burst, global stock markets crashed and the whole developed world was in the grip of the Great Depression. The resulting massive unemployment and human misery lasted until, perversely, economic stimulus was provided when the great economic powers in Europe and the New World re-armed.

There was widespread populist revulsion about the role that greed had played in creating an unsustainable and unstable economic system in which the few benefited at the cost of the many. In that context, intellectuals, academics, governments and others questioned the role of business in society and the degree to which business leaders should be held morally and even legally accountable for the impact of the decisions they make that have an impact on the health and welfare of the public.

Legal scholars, economists, policy makers and business-people started to analyze systematically whether business should play a role in shaping the broader political economy of nations. They asked whether business leaders should be co-opted into the process of policy-making or simply should be regulated and controlled by policy makers and legislatures. Those favoring corporatist solutions urged businesses to act "in the national interest" and were prepared to endorse a great deal of self-regulation by businesses. Those who were either more cynical or realistic, depending on one's perspective, felt that businesses must be regulated by government because they could not be trusted to act in anything other than their own narrowly defined self-interests.

The 1930s was also when "professional managers" began to be viewed as having interests both similar to and different from passive shareholders of companies. There were arguments for managers making pro-social decisions in the broad interest of the societies within which they operated. Counterarguments emphasized the strict fiduciary responsibility of managers to shareholders—a responsibility that did not allow them the luxury of deciding what was in the broader interest of society unless shareholders would clearly benefit from their doing so.

The arguments about the societal role of business have continued to this day. What has developed is a system in which businesses are generally free to pursue their own interests, with governments intervening on general concerns such as antitrust, environmental emissions, occupational health and safety, and the marketing of pharmaceuticals, and on other ad hoc issues where business activities affect the broader society and the macro-economy.

These different perspectives were to emerge after the Second World War in two philosophically distinct forms of capitalism. In some countries, notably the United States and the United Kingdom, capitalism became interpreted as the pursuit of shareholder value within the constraints of the law and associated regulations. In continental Europe, especially Germany, France and the Benelux countries, capitalism had a greater emphasis on balance between shareholder returns and the interests of other stakeholders in the enterprise, including employees, customers, suppliers, the communities affected by business decisions and, more recently, the planet.

At least until the recent recession it was generally conceded that the shareholder primacy form of capitalism had been more successful in generating real economic growth and employment than the European form of capitalism, even though it had resulted in more uneven distribution of incomes and wealth. The track record of the shareholder primacy model has been a source of frustration for those who saw greater social justice in the balanced stakeholder approach.

The Paradox

There has always been a paradoxical relationship between business corporations, particularly large ones, and the societies within which they operate.

On the one hand, businesses are welcomed for a variety of reasons: the investment they bring, the jobs they create, the products and services they produce, the support they give to local community groups, the taxes they pay to multiple levels of government and the opportunities they provide for people to live their lives with some confidence that their children will have good futures. Communities compete for this economic investment, and people in the developing world migrate from poor, rural farming communities to cities that develop a good economic and industrial base.

On the other hand, the general public is deeply suspicious of the motives of corporations. "Businesspeople" have never ranked highly in the esteem of the general public, despite certain individuals reaching iconic status. In early 2009, a British magazine reported that the public perception of bankers was worse than that of either lawyers or even politicians—a new nadir for the profession. In March 2010, Jamie Dimon, the CEO of JPMorgan Chase, complained bitterly about the demonization of bankers in the wake of the 2008 financial meltdown. At the same time, President Barack Obama was pushing through his healthcare reform using the public's anger with healthcare insurance companies as a principal lever to mobilize support.

Bankers are just the latest in a long line of business leaders to have come under attack. Among those who have been condemned by one group or another for their alleged social irresponsibility are the financiers of the Middle Ages, the robber barons of early American business, the mill-owners of the Industrial Revolution, promoters of dot.com stocks in the 1990s and hedge-fund operators and sub-prime loan packagers of more recent vintage. Also under fire from time to time: chemical and mining companies, oil refineries, data processing companies that outsource jobs to low-wage countries, airlines that help deplete the ozone layer, manufacturers and marketers of gas-guzzling cars and trucks, and companies that use non-recyclable packaging.

The Corporate Social Responsibility Movement

There have always been groups and individuals who have opposed the actions of corporations and, more generally, the capitalist economic system. Over the past 50 years a global corporate social responsibility (CSR) movement has been growing in both membership and influence. As with many social movements it is neither unified nor centrally planned. It is composed of many different groups and individuals with interests as diverse as the environment, human rights, employee rights, reduction of inequalities in wealth and income, social development, gender politics and international peace.

The movement has spawned multiple non-governmental organizations, institutes, agencies, research centers and chairs, ISO 14001 and 26000 standards, measurements of social performance, legislation and regulation, magazines, newsletters, blogs, conferences, social networks and, of course, a large consulting industry. These, in turn, provided the inputs and energy for the social movement to grow and develop.

While different groups have different goals, the thrust of members of this CSR movement is to change the relationship between corporations and the societies within which they operate. They see this change coming in a variety of ways, including through popularly supported legislation and regulation; by educating consumers so that they will reflect their social concerns in their marketplace decisions; and by persuading corporate directors, managers and employees to be more socially aware and act responsibly.

Corporations are becoming used to being attacked by advocates for various causes who bring pressure to bear through the established media and, more recently, through blogs, YouTube, Twitter and other social networks. The favorite targets of bloggers such as GreenMonk are large corporations like Nestle, Intel and Heineken. Bloggers praise those companies that take what they judge to be environmentally sound actions, censure those who do environmental damage and heap scorn on those who appear to be acting in a socially responsible way primarily for public relations purposes.

Advocacy organizations and other special interest groups have defined the term "corporate social responsibility" quite differently from members of the general public. A survey in 2006 showed that most people define CSR in very personal terms, using it to describe actions by companies that personally affect them or people they know. The majority of survey respondents thought companies were irresponsible when they treated employees poorly, when they shut down or relocated jobs to low-wage countries, or when there were local, visible impacts on the environment such as waste dumps or abandoned plants. Respondents also mentioned the positive contributions of companies to local communities such as their support of sports teams, community organizations, charitable causes, schools and colleges.

Business Response to the CSR Movement

Many businesses seem to be heeding the call to be more responsible. They seek to link their names with a variety of socially responsible actions such as developing smart electricity grids and wind farms, selling or serving "fair trade" coffee, supporting micro-lending in developing countries, sponsoring community service days, reducing the amount of salt in processed foods, abandoning the free distribution of plastic bags in food stores and other programs. More and more publicly listed firms are adding CSR reports to their annual reports. Others are having their CSR performance audited and evaluated. Companies are generally becoming more interested in being well regarded on the CSR dimension.

There are both cynics and skeptics about the response of business to CSR pressures. The cynics can't accept that business leaders would act in ways that served the interests of anyone but themselves and their shareholders. The skeptics ask, quite appropriately, if businesspeople are supporting CSR priorities only to look good in the eyes of their customers, employees or investors.

Advocates for a CSR approach urge business executives to pay good wages and provide good working conditions, be mindful of the environment, refrain from relocating businesses into more cost-competitive areas, support local community groups and do many other things that would make them "socially responsible." In return for pursuing a triple bottom-line (shareholders, employees and society/community), the advocates claim, these businesses will be "sustainable."

To buttress their position, CSR advocates present case studies of companies that have pursued their recommended approaches and prospered. They also identify a growing list of corporations, large and small, that have embraced many social causes, especially the preservation of the environment. Their logic is appealing. A corporation can be healthy in the long term only if its business environment is healthy. As a result, embracing social responsibility, they claim, is a "no-brainer."

Many of these advocates have little empathy for the very real pressures on business leaders to operate their businesses in globally competitive environments and to demonstrate consistently good short-term financial results and sustainable growth. They find it easy to pour scorn on the executive who does not decide in favor of the latest in "green" technology. They forget that such a decision may put the business at a competitive disadvantage and fail to draw additional business because the action has no immediate appeal to the customer base. Exhorting executives to take a long-term view ignores the reality of short-term requirements and pressures. After all, getting to the long term requires performance in the near term.

The Current Debate

This debate has moved out of the halls of academe and the political sphere and into popular culture. Gordon Gekko's infamous "greed is good" speech in the movie *Wall Street* sought to establish the pursuit of self-interest as something that was itself good for society. Gekko argued that it unleashed the full, feral intensity of hard-working, imaginative, competitive business leaders who create wealth and capture some of it for themselves.

Gekko's speech was a contemporary rendering of Milton Friedman's argument[1] that businesses should focus on doing what is good for themselves and leave it up to the marketplace,

---

1 Friedman, Milton, "The Social Responsibility of Business Is to Increase Its Profits," *The New York Times Magazine*, September 13, 1970.

governments, trade unions and other "market actors" to regulate what businesses do. Friedman argued that businesses are socially responsible when they do what they are supposed to do—make money for their shareholders. They should not assume the role of social arbiter and should refrain from deciding what is good or bad for society. That is the role of governments and other economic and political actors in society.

His was not a selfish argument but rather a moral one based on classical utilitarian reasoning. While recognizing that some people become wealthier than others as a result of the activities of business, Friedman was able to argue convincingly that the greatest good for the most people comes from a society in which business pursues profits and governments and other forces regulate business activities. However, his argument ignored the substantial asymmetries of information, knowledge, skills, power and resources between the leaders of business and those who were supposed to balance their excesses in the broader public interest.

In sharp contrast to the fictional but startlingly realistic Gordon Gekko, the very real Warren Buffett is the personification of the socially aware business leader who simply "gets" what the relationship between business leaders and society must be. On a *Charlie Rose* show, he acknowledged that he was rich because he was allowed to become rich by the society within which he operates. In his own words, "If I were stranded on a desert island I'd never make a nickel!" He went on to add that it would be fair to more heavily tax him, Bill Gates and other very wealthy businesspeople to deal with the consequences of recent financial and economic upheavals, given that they are the greatest beneficiaries of a capitalist society.

Buffett is not alone among business leaders in recognizing a simple fact of life: *Businesses have a conditional license to operate.* To the extent they meet the expectations of society they will be encouraged and allowed to operate freely. When they violate those expectations they will be regulated, controlled or even prevented from doing business, either by the behaviors of people in the marketplace or by governments and their agencies.

So it follows that, increasingly, business leaders are recognizing it's not wise to make a mess in their own backyard. They understand that by making their backyard a desirable place to be, it can draw people to the corporation, as customers, employees or investors. So, while caring for society is a virtuous endeavor, it is also an act of self-interest. This view differs, then, from the notion of greed in that it is not based solely on self-interest; it seeks to maximize self-gain while also benefiting others. The goal is to integrate or balance legitimate interests, whereas greed pursues self-interest without taking into account the interests of others.

Of course, some backyards are bigger than others. The individually owned business operating in one small town has a different set of responsibilities from Wal-Mart, General Electric or other multinational or global corporations. Much of the debate about the social responsibility of business has focused on large corporations, at least to date. However, more and more the owners and operators of small and medium-size businesses are being called to account for their impact on their communities and environments.

Social Responsibility and the Cross-Enterprise Leader

Today's business leaders must have a deep understanding of the case for and against businesses taking societal preferences and impact into consideration when making decisions. To constructively engage the critics and the supporters of business they must consider the case for business social responsibility as both a moral imperative and a sensible business decision in the interests of shareholders.

Even if their personal ideology rejects the concept that businesses should be concerned with anything other than shareholder returns in the short run, business leaders must accept that there *is* a vibrant and growing CSR movement—a movement that constantly changes its focus to different aspects of corporate activity and has access to public opinion through digital media and the Internet. Indeed, recent public opinion surveys indicate that people, especially young people, are more and more concerned with social issues and expect businesses to serve the needs of society.

Business leaders must identify the potential areas of interest that CSR organizations may have in their organizations and where there may be friction. This may involve reviewing product formulations, packaging, distribution processes, supply chain relationships, community involvement and many, many other areas. This is not a trivial exercise. More and more CSR groups have become expert at analyzing the social performance of businesses, detecting superficial responses to their concerns and exposing insincere attempts to address real issues.

Senior leaders can't do this unless their staffs, from senior executives to front-line employees, are sensitized to the issues and exposed to the views of stakeholders. They must understand the importance of both organized CSR groups and the more ephemeral public opinion. This requires formal education and training, discussion within companies, consultation with stakeholder groups and companies and antennae that are finely tuned to shifts in opinion around social issues.

Leaders also must decide what their stance will be with respect to these issues. In many situations, the response could range from being merely compliant with legislation and regulation to seeking to achieve social good beyond compliance or striving for standards of excellence. Non-compliance has consequences in terms of penalties, reputational damage and damaged relationships with employees, customers and other stakeholders. Many companies find that seeking social good and striving for excellence pays dividends in positive customer sentiment, more committed and motivated employees, and suppliers who work creatively with them to develop and market products that are superior to those offered by competitors who have less commitment to social responsibility.

But it would be irresponsible of business leaders to make such commitments without considering the impact on shareholders. An executive or manager in a company has a fiduciary obligation to act in the interests of the company and consequently the shareholders. In owner-managed companies the owners can decide what stance they will take on CSR issues because it's their money. In both cases it is incumbent on managers to consider seriously the short- and long-term benefits and costs of pro-social decisions.

Conclusion

The 11-year-old mission statement of the Richard Ivey School of Business is "To develop business leaders who think globally, act strategically and contribute to the societies within which they operate." There is nothing soft or sentimental about this statement. It reflects the reality that business enterprises live in symbiotic relationships with the societies in which they operate and have a vested interest in ensuring the health of those societies.

Whether awareness of social issues and pro-social actions is driven by moral conviction or crass financial interest is moot. Failing to recognize the role of business in society and take a stance on key social issues will lead almost certainly to poor analysis of business situations and poor decision-making. Good decision-making in today's business environment depends on cross-enterprise leaders who are committed to driving shareholder value, sensitized to social issues and trends, and creative in positioning their organizations on the right side of the issues. The future of the capitalist system that, for all its flaws, has delivered great benefits and is the hope for the developing world may depend on it.

~9~

Building Sustainable Value through Cross-Enterprise Leadership

BY TIMA BANSAL AND MICHAEL WOOD

Wal-Mart has made enormous strides toward environmental stewardship. On its corporate website, Wal-Mart claims that it wants to use only renewable energy, create no waste and sell products that sustain people and the environment. These aspirations are quite laudable. But, there's a rub. How can a company whose profits are directly tied to selling large volumes of low-cost product help to sustain the environment?

Such contradictions are endemic to business. In their endless pursuit of profits, firms inevitably need to choose between what's good for the firm and what's good for society. Such choices often come down to whose interests are most important—those of the firm's shareholders or those of its employees and its community.

For example, firms can save costs by paying employees as little as possible, or even by replacing expensive employees with cheaper ones. However, in the long run, such moves can tear at the firm's social fabric. Employees who are paid less may become less trusting, less committed and less productive. These cost-cutting measures may present false economies, but nevertheless, firms often take such actions.

There is an alternative. Firms could incur high short-term costs by offering generous employee compensation packages. Although there may be sacrifices in the short term, firms may reap long-term benefits through greater employee loyalty, lower turnover, improved motivation and creativity. The challenge is to manage for the short term while building for the long term. Firms that manage this duality within the firm, in other words, build sustainable value, are not as likely to see a trade-off between business and society.

Business schools have been critiqued for their reliance on theories that reinforce a myopic, short-term and self-interested approach to business.[1,2,3] By dissociating the firm from society, many business schools have encouraged such trade-off thinking between business and society.

At the Richard Ivey School of Business, faculty members believe their role is to encourage students to see a fuller picture of business decisions. The cross-enterprise leadership approach promotes a management perspective that extends beyond bar graphs and flowcharts to a fuller understanding of the far-reaching and long-lasting effects of business decisions and activities. Ivey's commitment to cross-enterprise leadership, however,

---

1 H. Mintzberg (March 16, 2009). "America's Monumental Failure of Management." *The Globe and Mail.*
2 J. M. Podolny (March 30, 2009). "Are Business Schools to Blame?" *Harvard Business Review.* Retrieved March 20, 2010, from http://blogs.hbr.org/how-to-fix-business-schools/2009/03/are-business-schools-to-blame.html
3 P. Stott (March 25, 2009). "A Crisis in MBA Culture?" CNBC. Retrieved March 20, 2010, from http://www.cnbc.com/id/29877474/A_Crisis_In_MBA_Culture

extends beyond just its pedagogy; in 2007, Ivey founded the Network for Business Sustainability to actively foster meaningful collaboration between academia and industry.

In this chapter, we suggest that cross-enterprise leadership provides an antidote to correct the ills of poor management practices. Businesses can be agents of positive change instead of the target of public criticism. But this management approach requires managers to broaden their horizon and to work toward building sustainable value. Rather than stripping the planet and its people in their pursuit of profits, firms can instead use their profits to build both for their firm and society. Although cross-enterprise leadership is only a part of the answer, we argue here that its role is significant.

What Is Sustainable Value?

The notion of sustainability gained traction soon after the World Commission on Environment and Development (WCED) articulated its view of sustainable development in 1987. The WCED defined sustainable development that "meet[s] the needs of the present without compromising the ability of future generations to meet their own needs."[4] Since then, business has tried to unpack the activities that constitute "sustainable value."

In our view, *firms are building sustainable value when they enhance economic, social and ecological systems.* In other words, they must contribute to the principles of economic efficiency, social equity and environmental integrity in their business decisions. A thumbnail sketch of some key issues associated with each of these principles is provided in Table 1.

---

4 World Commission on Environment and Development, *Our Common Future* (New York: Oxford University Press, 1987), 43.

TABLE 1: Issues Addressed through Sustainable Development

System	Guiding Principle	Issues
Economic	Efficiency	Innovation
		Prosperity
		Productivity
Social	Equity	Poverty
		Health and wellness
		Human rights
		Equitable sharing of resources and risk
Environment	Integrity	Climate change
		Land use
		Water quality and quantity
		Biodiversity
		Over-exploitation of resources

Source: United Nations Department of Economic and Social Affairs. (2009). Sustainable Development Topics. Retrieved March 19, 2010, from http://www.un.org/esa/dsd/susdevtopics/sdt_index.shtml

Why do firms choose to build sustainable value, especially given the pressures they are under to generate immediate high returns? Quite simply, sustainable value builds organizational resiliency. Because of the extra buffers and slack these firms build into their organization, they are better able to withstand shocks, whether financial meltdowns or product or process failures. Sustainable businesses are embedded in the community, so when these firms encounter adversity, the support of their powerful relationships can help them to bounce back. These firms invest in relationships, in their brand and in their social license to operate; these social assets help them not only to survive the bad times but also to thrive through the good times.

Generating sustainable value requires firms to integrate multiple perspectives, as illustrated by the metaphor in Figure 1.

Imagine a manager sitting at a table with three different stakeholders. Each tries to interpret the issue on the table. Depending on the perspective, the individual will see an M, E, W or 3. Each perspective is equally valid; no one perspective is superior to the others. The manager who seeks to build sustainable value will listen to each stakeholder's perspective, and through the dialogue, recognize the issue as multifaceted.

FIGURE 1: Building Sustainable Value by Seeing Different Perspectives

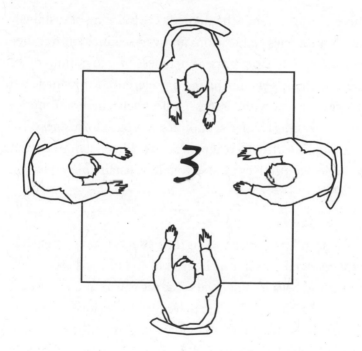

This ability to view issues from all sides acknowledges the complexity embedded in managerial decisions and is one of the hallmarks of cross-enterprise leadership. Cross-enterprise managers are more empathetic than managers who view issues from just one angle. They do not push their own perspective and ideas, but instead seek to solve complex problems creatively. They involve multiple stakeholders, even those who are on the fringe, and they are able to honor each stakeholder's contributions and perspectives. Diversity is embraced, not ignored. In doing so, the value created is more sustainable because it satisfies a wider set of stakeholders.

The Emphasis of Economics in Business and Business Education

There are three trends that impede the building of sustainable value in business education: an over-reliance on numbers, especially related to profits; an acquiescence to notions of self-interest and opportunism; and a preference for management theory over real-world issues. Collectively, these assumptions convey an almost hyper-economics approach to business. They result in a short-term orientation and blind managers to the multiple perspectives needed to build sustainable value.

The Relentless Pursuit of Profits

It is no wonder that firms focus their attention on profits; short-term financial value is much easier to quantify than sustainable value. And because financial value is easily reduced to a single number, financial value can drive firm behavior—so much so that profit has become the language of competition. It focuses the attention of managers and motivates them to act. Much like running a race, managers set their sights on measurable goals, aiming to lower costs, increase revenues, improve market share, build efficiencies or reduce turnover. Their single-minded focus on these numbers precludes paying attention to the softer issues that defy quantification, such as human health and satisfaction.

Not only do profits motivate, they are also easy to commu-nicate. A number carries the same meaning across languages and culture. A manager who generates $1 million in revenues for her firm in Canada only needs to convert the amount to yuan to be fully understood in China. In our pursuit to join the global economy, the international language of business has necessarily become firm profit.

Social issues, on the other hand, are embedded in language and culture. Whereas Canadians value multiculturalism as a societal ideal, in many other cultures diversity is not ac-knowledged as having value. For example, issues of gender and culture dominate the diversity discourse in Canada, whereas race tops the discourse in South Africa. Social issues do not follow simple rules that can be communicated efficiently in our globalized world. The pursuit for organizational efficiencies and globalization leaves little room for addressing social and environmental issues.

The Rhetoric of Self-Interest Becomes Reality

In an effort to develop elegant analytical models, economists made assumptions of human behavior. Building on Adam Smith's notions of the invisible hand, economic man was as-sumed to be rational, self-interested and opportunistic. Such assumptions would lead logically to Milton Friedman's argu-ment that a corporation's only social responsibility is to increase profits.[5]

However, Milton Friedman was not advocating for unbri-dled self-interested anarchy; rather, he was arguing for a strong and relevant government. He was also arguing that businesses

---

5 M. Friedman, "Social Responsibility of Business is to Increase Profits", *The New York Times Magazine*. September 13, 1970.

collectively behave *as if* they are self-interested. The collective, however, is not the same as each individual acting "unreservedly in [her own] own narrowly-defined self-interest[s]."[6] For example, when a gust of wind blows through a tree, all the tree's leaves appear to be pointing in the same direction. However, closer inspection will reveal considerable chaos, with many of the leaves stirred about in different directions. Collectively, though, the leaves seem to uniformly blow in the same direction.

As well, rationality is best viewed through the rear-view mirror. Economists are the strongest proponents of rationality, having coined the phrase "post hoc rationalization." Rationality and self-interest are useful assumptions when explaining behavior retrospectively, but these assumptions are woefully inadequate in predicting future behavior.

Traditionally, business schools have taken the ideas that were meant to both describe society as a whole and to explain past behavior and have paraded these ideas as relevant in predicting individual behavior. However, early economists had not intended for individuals to forsake social considerations in favor of their personal interests. Somewhere, however, things went awry. As a result, in too many business school hallways, one can hear Gordon Gekko's declaration in Oliver Stone's film *Wall Street*, "greed is good."

At risk is not only the assumption that everyone is opportunistic and self-interested but also the possibility that, based on this rhetoric, we will start to create our own reality. In fact, there is considerable evidence showing that business and economics students are more self-interested than other students.[7, 8, 9]

---

6 E. Noreen (1988). "The Economics of Ethics: A New Perspective on Agency Theory." *Accounting, Organizations, and Society*, 13: 359.
7 R. H. Frank, T. D.Gilovich and D.T. Regan (1993). "Does Studying Economics Inhibit Cooperation?" *Journal of Economic Perspectives*, 7(2): 159–171.
8 G. Marwell and R. E.Ames (1981). "Economists Free Ride, Does Anyone Else?" *Journal of Public Economics*, 15: 295–310.
9 D.T. Miller (1999). "The Norm of Self-Interest." *American Psychologist*, 54: 1053–1060

A recent simulation, for example, found that students trained in economics tended to keep more resources for themselves relative to students with no economics training.[10] Further, Miller argued in *American Psychologist* that "the experience of taking a course in microeconomics actually altered students' conceptions of the appropriateness of acting in a self-interested manner, not merely their definition of self-interest."[11]

The Fragmentation of Business and Business Curricula
As businesses become larger, more diversified and more global, they also become more fragmented, making the big picture increasingly difficult to see. And when the big picture is obscured, there is increasing risk that attention will focus on short-term profits and self-interests.

Consider this irony. An important ingredient in many green technologies, such as solar panels and hybrid vehicles, is dysprosium. This heavy, rare earth metal is extracted and processed almost exclusively in China. Miners scrape off topsoil and shovel the underlying clay into large pits in the ground, where acids are used to extract the valuable elements. The acid used in the extraction process ultimately washes into waterways, contaminating the water supply, in turn destroying rice paddies and fish farms on which the residents downstream depend.[12] So, in an effort to produce green technologies, the same firms contribute to environmental decay and the dislocation of local people.

When we deconstruct problems, such as by emphasizing the need for solar power without considering the source of the solar

10 J. R. Carter and M. D. Irons (1991). "Are Economists Different, and If So, Why?" *Journal of Economic Perspectives,* 5(2): 171–177.
11 D.T. Miller (1999). "The Norm of Self-Interest." *American Psychologist,* 54: 1055.
12 K. Bradsher (December 25, 2009). "Earth-Friendly Elements, Mined Destructively." *The New York Times.* Retrieved January 5, 2010, from http://www.nytimes.com/2009/12/26/business/global/26rare.html?_r=1&hp

panels, we incur the long-term risk of undermining the very goal that we aimed to accomplish in the short run. By parsing complex systems into discrete parts, we gain false confidence in our ability to predict outcomes. This process, called bracketing, assigns phenomena to discrete categories. However, phenomena can sometimes be assigned to the wrong categories, resulting in false characterizations, bad predictions and, most importantly, a failure to see the big picture. The characteristics of the smaller categories become the focus of attention, replacing a focus on the central issues.

The evidence for climate change, for example, has long been mounting. The data are drawn from multiple sources, including ice cores, ocean temperatures, tree rings and patterns of animal migration. Few people in the world see the big picture. The few who do, such as James Lovelock, argue that we are well past the tipping point and that a climate catastrophe is inevitable.[13] Scientists and businesspeople alike who view just a narrow slice of this issue are likely to underestimate the magnitude of the problem.

This fragmentation is also evident in business education and practice. Business decisions are bracketed into strategy, marketing, finance, organizational behavior, accounting, operations and so on. Managers often carry these silos into their organizations, resulting in poor decisions because the big picture is obstructed.

This fracturing of business education and practice impairs perspective, so that managers not only fail to acknowledge the impact of their decisions within and beyond the boundaries of their firms but also, and more importantly, fail to make effective decisions. Effective managers need to step back from the details and consider the big picture.

---

13 D. Aitkenhead (October 28, 2008). "Enjoy Life While You Can." *The Guardian*. Retrieved March 13, 2010, from http://www.guardian.co.uk/theguardian/2008/mar/01/scienceofclimatechange.climatechange

Cross-Enterprise Leadership Builds Sustainable Value

Cross-enterprise leadership starts with the issue, not with the solution, by acknowledging the interconnections among organizations, among functions and across time. Business issues cannot be assigned to silos, under the rubric of finance, accounting, marketing or operations. Instead, business issues span the entire organization, the entire supply chain, and the entire stakeholder community. Cross-enterprise leadership recognizes that today's success is dependent on future outcomes—and vice versa. This systems view is central to achieving sustainability and to effecting cross-enterprise leadership.

Robust economic systems require healthy societies that operate within the carrying capacity of the natural environment. In an interconnected system, failures in any one system, whether economic, social or environmental, could cascade into a systems failure.

The cross-enterprise leadership approach builds sustainable value through four main mechanisms:

1. By expanding the dimension of firm performance
2. By looking beyond boundaries and integrating knowledge from diverse perspectives
3. By appreciating the dynamic and complex environment
4. By building distributed, empowered and dynamic leadership

We describe each in detail below.

Broadening the View of Firm Success

In 2008, Mike Duke, President and CEO of Wal-Mart Stores Inc., while making a presentation in Beijing to an audience of more than 1,000 suppliers and NGO and government representatives, stated, "it's time to move forward with building a more socially and environmentally responsible supply chain. We are expecting more of ourselves at Wal-Mart and expecting more of our suppliers."[14] The mobilization of the resources of the world's largest retailer has the power to challenge other organizations to think beyond the traditional bottom line.

Cross-enterprise leadership forces firms to think about firm success, not just for each division but for the firm's position in society. Cross-enterprise leadership requires firms to recognize that they have stakeholders, and the success of the firm cannot be sustained if a stakeholder group with a legitimate interest in the firm's activities perceives its interests have been compromised because of the firm's activity. More so now than ever, even fringe stakeholder groups are finding mechanisms to voice their concerns—and to do so vociferously.

Success, then, does not merely attend to short-term profits. Success requires an understanding of sustained high performance and an understanding that draws the community into the firm's operations so that the community is then deeply involved.

Seeing the Big Picture

In 2007, Gap Inc. subcontracted its clothing production; the subcontracted organizations, in turn, exploited children for their cheap labor. Although the problem resided in another organization, customers tend not to differentiate between a company and its suppliers. Gap executives responded quickly when they became aware of the situation, but the company's reputation as a leader in ethical sourcing was already damaged.[15]

14 Wal-Mart Canada, Corporate Social Responsibility Report, July 2009.
15 D. McDougall (October 28, 2007). "Child Sweatshop Shame Threatnens Gap's Ethical Image." *The Guardian*. Retrieved March 11, 2010, from http://www.guardian.co.uk/business/2007/oct/28/ethicalbusiness.india

To be able to accurately assess the multiple dimensions of performance, issues must be viewed from all angles and from all places (as illustrated in Figure 1 on page 175). Cross-enterprise leadership recognizes that departmental, firm, cultural and knowledge boundaries can restrict a comprehensive under-standing. That is, organizations must look beyond the narrow definition of "profit" to accurately assess risks and identify opportunities.

Recognizing the Dynamic Complexity of Business Systems

When oil prices began their upward climb in 2005, ethanol became an increasingly desirable additive to gasoline because of its low-cost ability to improve energy output. But the greater attention on corn resulted in both oil, at US$145 per barrel, and corn, at US$8.07 a bushel,[16] reaching all-time high prices in the summer of 2008. More insidious, however, was that corn was being redirected from the kitchen table to the gas tank, further aggravating poverty.[17]

Systems are dynamic and complex. Changing one element in the system causes knock-on effects to other elements of the system. Predicting the repercussions in non-linear systems is challenging, and often impossible. Cross-enterprise leadership, however, encourages a holistic approach to organizations, the environment and society. Given its emphasis on the big picture, cross-enterprise leadership helps to avoid some of the errors made through bracketing and reductionism. It forces managers to take an inside look at the problem, but then to pull back and place the issue in the context of the big picture.

---

16 Reuters Bloomberg (June 16, 2008). "Floods Push U.S. Corn Prices to Records." *The New York Times*. Retrieved March 17, 2010, from http://www.nytimes.com/2008/06/16/business/worldbusiness/16iht-corn.1.13735103.html
17 C. F. Runge (2010). "The Case Against Biofuels: Probing Ethanol's Hidden Costs." Retrieved March 16, 2010, from http://e360.yale.edu/content/feature.msp?id=2251

Building Distributed, Empowering and Dynamic Leadership

In 2007, Wal-Mart started a program called the Personal Sustainability Projects to empower its 80,000 associates to generate ideas for reducing the organization's environmental footprint and to reach out to the community. To date, Wal-Mart reports more than 60,000 projects have been developed, far exceeding its goal of 25,000.[18] As this overwhelming response demonstrates, people want to be engaged and want to take action to make a difference.

Leadership in a sustainable environment differs from the more conventional top-down hierarchical forms that we often envision. Leadership in a sustainable environment tends to be distributed throughout an organization. People within the organization will champion ideas that form the collective identity of the organization. By associating leadership with ideas and distributing them throughout the organization, people are empowered to own the ideas and shape the organization. The organization, then, is not merely a collection of individuals working as part of a production system but becomes a cohesive group of people who share a vision and goal that extends beyond money and involves the firm's connections to society. The diversity of ideas opens the organization to new concepts and helps the organization to respond quickly to impending threats.

Leadership in sustainable organizations, then, is not about being different from or better than the rest; instead, it is about leading from within and displaying energy through agency. These leaders will ebb and flow in their visibility as their ideas that were new last week are replaced by newer ideas today. Unlike conventional forms of leadership, which are focused

---

18 Wal-Mart Canada Corporate Social Responsibility Report, July 2009.

on directing, cross-enterprise leaders are skilled at learning, developing and influencing others.

Building Sustainable Value at Ivey

At the Richard Ivey School of Business, the Centre for Building Sustainable Value embodies cross-enterprise leadership. Its vision is for Ivey to be recognized as a world leader in sustainability research and teaching and as a major force for positive change. The Centre embodies this vision through teaching, research and outreach. In this section, we describe one of its most ambitious initiatives, the Network for Business Sustainability, which puts into action some of the ideas described earlier in this chapter.

To tackle some of these most thorny social, environmental and economic issues, we need collective and concerted effort. Climate change, for example, poses one of the most significant challenges confronting mankind. This challenge, arguably, is greater than prior threats, such as nuclear holocausts and epidemics, because of the high uncertainty associated with positive feedback loops and the time lags in both the impacts and their solutions. A further challenge imposed by climate change is that both business and households create greenhouse gas emissions. No industry or household is exempt. We need a coordinated solution that involves industry, government and civil society.

However, as with any thorny issue, there will be winners and losers. In most cases, heavy industry and primary goods producers have the most to lose. As a result, each business easily can become entrenched in its own partisan interests. However, such entrenchment leads to immobility and inaction. The climate crisis will not be deflected. What we need, then, is a bipartisan agent—an organization that can assemble people with disparate positions and engender dialogue that focuses on innovative solutions, not entrenched positions.

We believe business schools are well placed to encourage such dialogue. Business schools can facilitate bipartisan participation by introducing evidence and research to the discussion. Businesses then can rise above their existing positions to creatively work toward potential solutions. As well, business schools are sympathetic to the needs of business and the value business brings to society. Business schools are empathetic to short-term demands while mindful of keeping an eye on long-term implications. They can bring a necessary level-headedness to these issues in a way that few others can.

The Network for Business Sustainability

The Network for Business Sustainability was designed to respond to these challenges. Founded in 2007 at the Richard Ivey Business School, the Network comprised more than 800 researchers, managers and students by 2010. Its mission is to enable business sustainability by fostering collaboration between industry and academia. It does so by building community, exchanging knowledge and spurring innovation. Collectively, the knowledge dormant in business schools and within organizations can help shape business practices and government policy. Ultimately, such collaboration, by using knowledge as the medium of exchange, can build sustainable value.

Approximately 40 percent of the $20 billion spent annually on research in Canada is conducted within universities. However, much of that research remains within the ivory towers. Imagine if we could harness those insights meaningfully, so that they could shape practice. Canada's competitiveness could leapfrog forward through sustainable business practices, which could provide a sustained competitive advantage.

Such a cross-enterprise leadership approach is in demand. The Network's new website (nbs.net) was launched in September 2009; by January 2010, it rose to the top of Google's hit list when searching for "business sustainability." By bringing together a community of researchers and practitioners, we are able to add meaningfully to a discourse that is helping to break down the silos within corporations, across corporations and between corporations and other sectors.

A powerful example is a meeting hosted in 2007 at the Network. In this meeting, a representative of Toronto-Dominion Bank, one of Canada's largest banks, was sitting adjacent to a representative from the Pembina Institute, a policy think tank committed to addressing climate change. The meeting initiated a dialogue that lasted almost a year. As a consequence, TD Bank announced that it would be the first Canadian bank to become carbon neutral. This move was a radical shift for a major Canadian bank and is likely to initiate significant changes within the industry.

So how does the Network break down the silos? First, we try to find a common language. Managers speak colloquially, aiming to be understood as simply and quickly as possible. Researchers, on the other hand, speak esoterically, in a tongue that must be respectful of norms that have taken time to evolve. Finding a common language that respects both groups is difficult, and it is easy for one group to dismiss the other. The Network aims to find a common platform through documents and events that can be understood by both groups in order to achieve practice-based research and research-based practice.

Second, we reach out to the community through various media. We use push and pull systems, through websites, newsletters and e-mails. We use social media, such as Facebook, Twitter and LinkedIn. And we hold events so that people can meet face-to-face. At each of these events, we encourage people from disparate and diverse communities to attend.

Finally, and most importantly, we co-produce knowledge with representatives from the corporate, non-profit, and academic communities through the following four-step process.

Stage 1: Setting Knowledge Priorities
The Leadership Council, which comprises up to 20 diverse representatives from business, government and non-profit organizations, meets annually for a full day to identify what they believe are the research priorities most relevant to the community of practice.

Stage 2: Synthesizing Knowledge
The Network commissions researchers to systematically review prior research in the top two priorities. The remaining priorities are communicated to the research community to spur on additional research.

Stage 3: Exchanging Knowledge
The Network widely communicates the findings of both studies through electronic media, conventional media and events.

Stage 4: Extending Knowledge
Recognizing that knowledge is not static, new academic research is translated into easy-to-skim, one-page research insights that are posted on our website and can be shared among managers.

We believe that this process embodies the notions of cross-enterprise leadership. We are shaping the field so that knowledge crosses the boundaries of research and practice and is driven by issues, not by the functional silos in which prior knowledge is embedded.

How Businesses Can Build Sustainable Value through Cross-Enterprise Leadership

Numerous learnings can be applied to all businesses through the example provided by the Network.

1. Have a Long-Term Vision

In business schools we hear a lot about vision, but maintaining that vision is necessary in all business decisions. In the day-to-day grind, we can too easily forget to filter our activities through this vision. But keeping the long-term vision in full view helps us to see the big picture. Consequently, we don't focus our attention on the present, so our vision of the future is always constrained by our present position. Instead, we focus on the possibilities of the future and decide what we need to do today to realize that future.

2. Engage the Community

Although the Network is, by definition, a group of loosely connected people, this same model is increasingly being used in business. As a result, more organizations do not have hard boundaries but soft ones, in which members of the community can come in and out. Employees volunteer in the local community on company time, and community members can engage in a business' decision-making processes. Using a Network model to think about your organization will help to ensure that you stay relevant.

3. Encourage Diversity

Diversity is not just about ensuring politically correct demographics. Diversity invites criticism and feedback. It is in the face of adversity that the most creative solutions are generated—solutions that will force multiple perspectives and that will reach for sustainability.

4. Co-create Products and Services

No business needs to go it alone. By involving employees, customers and the community to help develop products, you will create products that are not only more relevant, but also are more sustainable.

5. Distribute Leadership Throughout the Organization

The Network does not forward the interests of any one business school or any one corporation. The Network is egalitarian and democratic, both in form and in structure. In this way, we judge based on the quality of the ideas, not on status. Similarly, organizations that value ideas, no matter where they gestate, can maintain an energy and vitality that will always help to renew the organization.

Conclusion

Traditional business curriculum emphasizes competition. It encourages differentiating, focusing and seeking cost-efficiencies. It also encourages us to approach the messiness of business decisions by taking apart the issues, by deconstructing and bracketing them.

However, in doing so, we tend to compartmentalize and make trade-offs. We see black and white, rather than shades of gray. We are lulled into a false sense of security by the numbers generated through reams of equations, analyses and assumptions. Based on these rather tenuous numbers, we make strategic decisions.

This chapter has argued that most managers have been trained to see a narrow short-term perspective. We highlighted three consequences of this short-term, heavily economics-based perspective: a narrow focus on firm profits, an assumption that everyone is self-interested and the fragmentation of business education along disciplinary lines. As a result of these consequences, managers often assume that business can succeed only at the cost of social and environmental systems. Widening the focus allows managers both to see the big picture and to build sustainable value.

Cross-enterprise leadership holds promise for addressing the most intractable problems that we confront in our economy, environment and society. We offered several mechanisms through which to make this happen, by expanding the dimension of firm performance; by looking beyond boundaries and integrating knowledge from diverse perspectives; by appreciating the dynamic and complex environment; and by building distributed, empowered and dynamic leadership. The Network for Business Sustainability is one such example that helps to build sustainable value through cross-enterprise leadership.

For our population, our planet cannot sustain our present consumption patterns. We have reached our limits to growth. We need a new business model, one that embraces sustainability. Business must be part of the solution, not part of the problem.

~10~

Leadership on Trial

BY JEFFREY GANDZ, MARY CROSSAN, GERARD SEIJTS, STEPHEN SAPP
AND MARK VANDENBOSCH

Launched under the auspices of the Leading Cross-Enterprise
Research Centre, the "Leadership on Trial" initiative was designed to extract leadership lessons from the economic crisis
with a view to raising the practice of current and future business leadership. The near meltdown of the financial markets
in 2008 and the subsequent liquidity crisis and credit crunch
that exacerbated a global recession that started around the end
of 2007 served to focus attention on the quality of leadership
in major institutions and organizations. There were examples
of poor leadership that resulted in the collapse of many businesses and the accumulation of massive public debt. There were
examples of outstanding leadership that allowed organizations
to avoid major catastrophes, and that has positioned many of
them for subsequent successful growth.

In the period September 2009 to May 2010, we held a series of 11 focus-group discussions with groups of 15–25 CEOs and C-Suite executives in several Canadian cities, New York, London (U.K.) and Hong Kong. We also presented and discussed our findings with professionals involved in leadership development in major corporations and the public sector, both individually and in groups. Finally, we involved groups of business students at various levels in discussing our research findings and tentative conclusions as they emerged from the data analysis.

As facilitators at these forums, we advised participants that we were open minded but not empty minded and thus the authors of this chapter pooled their collective experience in strategy, leadership, finance, marketing, human resource management and the global environment of business to capture a very cross-enterprise perspective on leadership as it related to the economic crisis. The article was extremely well received and served the intended purpose of seeding the leadership forums and allowing us to delve even more deeply into the leadership challenges exposed by the crisis. The following is the article in its entirety, with a few minor revisions to match the format of this book. Preliminary insights from the leadership forums corroborated our analysis. A more detailed account of our findings will be forthcoming in a separate volume devoted to the project.

Introduction

In the aftermath of the near-collapse of the global economy in 2007–2009, the leadership of private and public sector organizations is being put on trial in the media, in congressional and parliamentary hearings, commissions of enquiry in legislatures around the world, in individual and class action lawsuits and in the courts of public opinion.

For those of us involved in the development of next generation leaders—whether we are executives, academics or leaders
in the public and not-for-profit sectors—there is a need for
some soul-searching. There are four basic questions that we
need to ask:

1.   What went wrong with leadership that contributed to the
     2008–2009 financial crisis and the devastation to people,
     organizations and national economies that followed it?
2.   Was this problem with leadership confined to the few
     organizations at the epicenter of the financial meltdown,
     or did this crisis reveal more broadly based problems with
     leadership in both private and public sectors?
3.   What can we learn from those organizations and leaders
     who anticipated the crisis and avoided it completely, or
     who coped well throughout the last couple of years and
     are therefore in good shape to benefit from the recovery?
4.   What more do we need to do, or do differently, to prepare
     the current generation of leaders to deal with the kinds of
     challenges that we have seen corporations, governments
     and not-for-profit organizations face in the last couple of
     years and those—as yet unknown—that they will face in
     the future?

We don't have all the answers to these questions, but we have
some thoughts about them that we want to share and that we
hope will stimulate dialogue. The end product will be a more
complete analysis and set of recommendations for the development of next-generation leaders by influencing the programs
they take, the experiences they get within their organizations
and the coaching and mentoring that will help them prepare

for the inevitable challenges that will confront them in their future leadership roles.

The Blame Game

There is much blame to be shared for the creation of the combustible mixture of excessive leverage in both consumer and financial markets, the credit market collapse and the conditions that ignited the bursting of the housing bubble leading to the recession and credit crises of 2008–2009 and the worst global recession since the 1930s.

There were covetous consumers who bought what they clearly could not afford should interest rates increase. There were pandering politicians who responded to their constituents' desires with non-sustainable macro- and microeconomic policies that encouraged the expansion of credit and home ownership at cheap interest rates and who acceded to the demands of the Wall Street and city investment bankers through the passage of legislation that in effect removed derivatives from regulatory oversight.[1]

There were bountiful bankers who made dubious credit decisions, especially in consumer lending, with zero-down and principal repayment only mortgages, and equity lines of credit based on volatile house prices, and there were enterprising entrepreneurs ready and willing to capitalize on the easy credit situation by arranging mortgage loans for fees and then passing the risk onto other parties. There was egregiously excessive executive compensation that in many documented cases was unrelated to the long-term risk that accrued to shareholders, suppliers, customers and eventually to the public purse, and

---

[1] The *Financial Services Modernization Act* (1999) was passed by both houses of congress on the last day of the Clinton administration.

there were delinquent directors who failed to govern in the interests of companies and their shareholders, paying excessive compensation to executives and managers, without regard to the risk to shareholders.

There were relaxed regulators who should have been more vigilant, especially with respect to the activities of certain hedge funds, naked short-sellers and the marketing of complex derivatives whose promoters were not the guarantors of their liquidity. These regulators' responses to "irrational exuberance" were to stoke the fires of demand with low interest rate policies. And, of course, there were the 24-hour news media and financial babble shows that zeroed in on every fact and rumor, magnifying and amplifying them while, at the same time, expressing horror at the panic their reports induced.

As explanations emerge as to what caused the recent financial crisis and deepened the recession that had already started, there is an overwhelming emphasis on the failure of "the system." One can read analyses from politicians, academics, executives and journalists that never even mention personal culpability. It's as if the great American comedian, Flip Wilson, were back again: His inevitable excuse for his own misdeeds was "The devil made me do it!"

There is no doubt that "the system" came close to a meltdown. But to blame "the system" risks diminishing the personal leadership failures of those who were charged with guiding their organizations and, in the case of the public servants, their economies through these challenging times. Unless we look at these mistakes we cannot learn from them. If we are to learn anything from this situation, we must focus on individual, group, organizational and systemic causes, learning both from those organizations that failed and those that avoided failure, even though they may have been sideswiped by the economic impact.

It also would be a mistake to focus only on the financial services industry. While the failures of Bear Sterns and Lehman Brothers and the near-failure of AIG, Citi, Bank of Scotland and many other banks and insurance companies were at the epicenter of the storm, firms in the broader "Main Street" economy also demonstrated stress fractures. Giants such as General Motors and Chrysler were hit hard, but they were just the most visible casualties among thousands of businesses around the world that seemed unable to withstand a recession that in no developed country saw GDP fall more than 7 percent from its peak, albeit one that was longer than any seen since the 1930s. For example, business bankruptcies in the United States rose 42.5 percent in the 12 months ended June 2008 over the previous 12 months and then rose again, this time by 62.7 percent, in the 12 months ended June 2009. Increases of similar magnitude were experienced in the U.K., and all OECD countries had significant increases in business and personal bankruptcies related to the slowdown in their economies.

What Impressed

With all that went wrong, there was also a lot that was impressive about how leaders acted during this period.

There were those financial institutions and individuals— executives, managers, directors and investors—who did not get caught up in the hype and excesses of the financial markets of the last decade and will get through this current mess reasonably unscathed. The leadership in these organizations approached this catastrophe-in-waiting with good, practical common sense and a principled approach to risk management.

They didn't get involved with what they did not understand, either as investors or sellers of investment products to others. They understood the boundary between reasoned and reasonable risk and reckless endangerment of their own and their investors' capital. They didn't allow past successes to blind them to the risks in every new decision, thereby avoiding personal overconfidence and hubris as well as team and organizational groupthink, the silent killers of good decision-making.

They resisted the criticism, even the chastisement of others, that they were missing opportunities, underperforming their peers or being too risk-averse. This was certainly true of the Canadian banks who, in the run-up to the events of 2008, were routinely characterized as underperforming. They understood that you don't get something for nothing in this world, that increased reward comes with increased risk, and they resisted the alchemists' claims that lead could be turned into gold, or a bunch of sub-prime mortgages could be turned into investment grade assets.[2]

They recognized that while hormones are good, when it comes to investing, neurons are better! They curbed the desire of many of their less experienced and aggressive staff to get involved in the more complex financially engineered products. They developed sensible policies and procedures by which they would screen products, and they kept reasonable controls on the actions of less experienced staff.

Businesses as a whole headed into this crisis with balance sheets in pretty good shape. They had not taken on a mountain of debt as they experienced some good years in the 2003–2007 period even as they coped with significant commodity inflation, especially in energy prices. Most developed-country

---

2 Canadian banks were subject to more stringent capital requirements than their U.S. counterparts, and it could be argued that this regulatory framework was what prevented them from going down the same route as many of the money-center banks in the U.S.

governments—with the notable exception of the United States—also had been reducing their annual deficits and accumulated debt levels, with many of them, including Canada, clearly anticipating that the good times would not last forever and that prudent fiscal management was a necessity.

The response to the financial and economic crisis also brought out some extraordinary leadership from the public sector as well as levels of international cooperation that had not been seen in many a decade. Both the political and administrative branches of governments around the world demonstrated an ability to work together with their international counterparts to handle a situation that had never been modeled before and that could well have left them paralyzed. Despite deep ideological rifts and personal hostilities fanned by eight years of an increasingly partisan and latterly unpopular administration in the U.S., Congress came together to pass emergency measures designed to prevent a deepening recession sliding into a depression. Governments in the OECD countries as well as emerging economies such as China, India and Brazil did their parts to form a common front to deal with a global economic recession by providing promise of stimulus and, even more important in the short run, by propping up their failing banks and insurance companies.

In what was certainly their finest hour, Ben Bernanke at the U.S. federal reserve and Henry Paulson at the Treasury department did what they were loathe to do yet had to do—bail out the major money-center and investment banks with injections of capital and various guarantees to the point that the world got the message. They would not be allowed to fail, there would be liquidity in the system, banks would be provided the capital to lend and the credit market seize-up would be unlocked.

An incoming and popular U.S. administration accepted the wisdom of doing this from an outgoing and deeply unpopular one and restored some confidence in the U.S. financial system, fully aware of the huge liability this would impose on their new regime. This action was repeated in the United Kingdom and most countries of the EU. Many of these actions were deeply un-popular and for good reason. There are those today who believe that reinforcing the fact that there are financial institutions that are too big to fail has created a moral hazard that will almost ensure that the recent history will repeat itself. Yet it had to be done. And the new regime carried on to bail out General Motors and Chrysler, fully aware of the implications of the collapse not only of those companies but the whole supply chains for the automobile companies (including Ford and transplants) and the need to see the maintenance and gradual transformation of these supply chains under orderly bankruptcies.

This sequence of events was played out in many other countries. In Canada, one can argue that the Conservative government of Prime Minister Harper was woefully slow to recognize the oncoming recession; however, when they did, they took immediate and significant action to demonstrate their resolve to stimulate the economy. Chancellor Merkel did the same in Germany, President Sarkozy did so in France, as did Prime Minister Brown in the U.K. The G20 meetings that took place in November 2008 and April 2009 stabilized a tot-tering global financial system and laid the groundwork for the recovery that is slowly but steadily starting to take hold.

The fact that it was many of the same leaders who failed to see the warning signs of the impending financial and economic crisis, who then acted to fix the problems and openly acknowl-edge their errors, says something important about leadership.

As long as leaders are human they will make mistakes. That they could come to terms with those mistakes, that they could use their vast knowledge and experience of economic history and the workings of the global financial system[3] to address an emergent crisis without being paralyzed by their preconceptions and ideologies, speaks volumes about the need for leaders to be intensely pragmatic and to be able to bring their intelligence and experience to bear in the contexts within which they have to lead.

Predictable Crises

Both the recession and the credit seize-up of 2008–2009[4] were among the most forecast and predictable events in recent economic history, although the magnitude and the ferocity of the economic storm unleashed by their interaction was greater than most people had anticipated.

In the 1990s respected economists and others were writing about the structural deficit in the United States resulting from persistent trade imbalances and fiscal entitlement programs. In the early part of this decade there were many books and articles pointing out the problems with mounting consumer credit card and bank debt, especially in the form of home equity loans. The massive and rapidly mounting leverage in the financial system was clearly apparent, as were the conspicuous bubbles in the property and commodity markets. And no lesser person than Alan Greenspan pointed out the "irrational exuberance" in the financial markets.[5]

---

3 The fact that Ben Bernanke was a world-class scholar specializing in the Great Depression and Henry Paulson was a former CEO of Goldman Sachs—the company that was at the very heart of the financial leveraging that took place in the 2000–2007 period—meant that there was no shortage of expertise in the financial leadership in the U.S.
4 The current evidence suggests that the recession in the U.S. actually began in mid-2007 but was not recognized as such until early 2008, a consequence of the technical definition of a recession as two quarters in a row of declining Gross Domestic Product.
5 The definition of "irrational exuberance" has its origin in a speech Alan Greenspan gave on December 5, 1996.

While there is never unanimity among economists,[6] the consensus in the writings of leading economists in 2006–2007 was that the good times of the last few years could not continue to roll forever, that there would be sharp retrenchments in the housing markets in the U.S., the U.K. and other OECD countries, and that the wealth effect of rapidly rising house prices that had encouraged consumers to get themselves deeper and deeper into debt for consumer goods and to make investments in real assets or financial assets at inflated prices must come to an end … soon. The problems with sub-prime mortgages had been identified even though the extent to which the securitization and insurance of those securities had grown was not widely recognized.

Within the smaller, but nevertheless substantial, investment banking business—employing tens of thousands of people in large and small financial centers around the world—the interconnectedness of the commercial banking system with the investment banking system also was known. They were, after all, the providers of the liquidity for most of these securitized assets and also were those who were arranging the insurance against risk in the form of credit default swaps and other financial backstops. There is an abundance of evidence that many in this industry knew of the fragility of the system and the increasing likelihood of a crash.[7]

Within the broader financial community there were many, many people who understood the problem with unregulated hedge fund activity, securitization of questionable mortgages, car loans and credit card receivables and the games that were being played with managing the associated risk with credit

---

6 A fact that caused President Harry Truman to call for a one-armed economist to avoid them saying, "on the one hand this, on the other hand that."
7 Some of the clearest evidence of this is in the transcripts of testimony given by the ratings agencies to Representative Henry Waxman's Energy and Commerce Committee in 2008.

default swaps that were themselves dependent on the good times continuing to roll. This was so obvious to insiders in the financial services industry that many of them—the five largest Canadian banks, for example—steered well clear of these types of investments or limited their involvement to amounts that were manageable with their capital reserves.

Many people were asking how Icelandic banks, for example, could have grown so rapidly despite the small size of the Icelandic economy and its lack of membership in the European Union. The answer was equally obvious—they were taking on enormous counter-party risks with nowhere near the capital reserves required to handle any crisis of confidence in the banking system. Unlike the Canadian banks, they were in way over their heads.

The problems with the economy were not confined to the financial services industry. The gross over-capacity in the automobile industry had been remarked on by many observers who pointed out that the 16 million plus units manufactured in the United States in 2007 were simply not warranted by the long-term trend line of customer purchases and leases and real wage increases, which had not been rising significantly through the previous decade. It was obvious that this volume of sales could be attributable only to the impact of easily available credit and lease terms backed by an assumption that debt-servicing costs could be met from wealth accumulation. People were talking openly about the need to reduce capacity by as much as 20 percent to 30 percent.[8]

Within many countries the decline in the U.S. dollar was also recognized as a severe threat to exports, perhaps no more so than in Canada, which had seen the Canadian dollar move

---

8 Mark Milner, ed., "Put the Brakes On, Car Firms Told: Global Overcapacity Risk Revealed," *The Guardian*, January 7, 2005.

from US$0.64 in 2002 to US$1.09 in 2007, obliterating the labor and benefits cost advantage for Canadian manufacturers
shipping into the U.S. Fiscal deficits and continuing U.S. trade
were sending alarm signals to employers and governments
alike ... but the warnings appeared to be falling on deaf ears as
Canadian productivity continued to lag pitifully behind that
of its major trading partner. Individuals, institutions, as well
as government reports pointed out this productivity gap in
manufacturing and services. But the response of senior leaders
at all levels was anemic at best. Perhaps they were blinded by
aggregate economic statistics that, because of the global boom
in commodity prices, especially oil and gas, made the Canadian
economy appear to be strong.

The pressure on employment levels in many OECD countries with historically strong manufacturing bases was already
severe before the economic downtown. The growth of global
sourcing, the drive by companies to source product from the
absolutely lowest cost parts of the world, was an opportunity
afforded by globalization but also reduced manufacturing employment in high-wage, developed economies, leaving them
highly vulnerable. By the early part of the decade, it was evident
that service jobs were going the same way with the massive
expansion of offshore call centers, the outsourcing of engineering, information technology, accounting work and other
professional services amounting to the loss of some $50 billion
in information services from the U.S. alone in 2008.[9]

This "rush to the bottom"[10] was creating wealth in developing countries and for some sectors—the owners, shareholders
and highly paid executives of the outsourcing firms and the

9 Rod Bourgeois, a technology services specialist at Sanford C. Bernstein & Company, quoted in
the New York Times, January 2009.
10 A term used to describe the migration of work and jobs from areas of high labor costs, rigid
labor markets and strict environmental regulations to developing countries that lack these constraints on manufacturing and, more recently, service industries.

outsourcers—but it was having a depressing impact on the salaries and wages paid in domestic firms. Real wages failed to increase significantly in areas such as manufacturing from 1980 to the present day, despite increases in productivity. Many were asking the question: Who was going to be earning the salaries and wages required to pay off the huge mortgages on inflated properties acquired at a time of rising expectations? Not in India or Ireland, but in Toronto, Cleveland, Philadelphia and Phoenix.

What Happened to the Radars?

If this was a predictable crisis, what happened to our ability to both detect and act on it? For more than 40 years, managers and executives have been urged to pay attention to the political, economic, societal and technological environments within which they operate. Such PEST analysis forms a key component of business school courses, in-company executive development programs and is supported by a plethora of conferences, programs, websites, blogs and other information services.

Yet in the run-up to this crisis, these radars seemed to have been disabled for many. It was as if many of the captains of industry were steering their boats by looking at their wakes rather than by looking forward. Seemingly mesmerized by their recent achievements they seemed unable to see the coast ahead, the dangers that lay in pursuing "last quarter plus more" goals through strategies that called for no reconsideration, even in the face of a rapidly deteriorating environment.

Have we, as leadership developers, been inadequate in the education and training we have provided in the tools of environmental analysis, or have we simply been ineffective in stressing its importance? Within companies, has this type of "external" analysis been restricted to so few people—the strategic planning group, for example—that most next-generation leaders are not getting exposure to this way of thinking? Have we tipped the scales so much toward execution and the art of the deal that we have minimized the importance of strategic analysis, risk assessment, contingency planning and scenario exploration?

Risk Analysis and Mitigation

The reason that we need radar is that we know—or reasonably ought to know—that there *are* risks out there.

Individuals took huge risks in the last 10 years, loading up on consumer debt through mortgages, rotating credit card balances and home equity loans in ways that defied historical limits of prudent behaviors. This all was stimulated by the "wealth effect" of rising property prices, even though income from employment was not increasing significantly. Individuals were opening margin accounts for financial assets and were invested increasingly in the higher-risk equity markets when their age and life circumstances would have counseled investment in lower-risk fixed income assets.

Many business organizations and governments that created and ran the regulatory processes over the last couple of decades operated in ways that were seemingly oblivious to the risks being run—whether this was the market risk that all organizations face, the reputational risk of marketing high-risk products to customers without the appetite or wherewithal to bear this risk, the strategic risk of investing in greater capacity in an overcapacity industry such as automotive assembly, or the operational risk associated with offshoring critical functions or running extended supply chains. It included the risk to the very foundations of the capitalist economic system being driven by the massive increases in leverage by individual consumers and financial institutions that were financing this consumer borrowing.

Regulators and politicians took risks in providing the enormous liquidity required to fuel this risk-taking through low interest rates, the reduction in difficulty of obtaining mortgage financing and the failure to regulate the derivatives and hedge fund markets in full knowledge of the rapid growth of those markets, albeit not really understanding the implications for systemic risk of that rapid growth of opaque and obscure markets.

The three key principles of risk management are simple: Don't take risks that you don't understand, make sure that you properly price risk, and never risk what you cannot afford to lose. Many in key leadership roles in our society violated all three of these.

One hypothesis that cannot be discounted is that, as educators and leadership developers, we have not given sufficient attention to understanding risk and risk management in our curricula and in the key experiences we give people who are on leadership development tracks in organizations. We tend to disaggregate risk: Finance professors talk about market and financial risk with little or no reference to reputational risk; marketing professors talk about brand and reputational risk but seldom in the same breath as financial risk; operations professors talk about operational risk and so on. Yet we seldom pull this all together, and compartmentalizing the subject leads to minimizing its importance.

A second hypothesis is that the assessment of risk and the robustness of strategies for its management have become extremely technical subjects, especially when it comes to market risk and the risk associated with various kinds of financial products. It may not be hard to understand the concept of a credit default swap, but it requires considerable knowledge and facility with complex formulae and algorithms to understand whether a pattern of credit default swap transactions makes sense for a specific company in a specific situation. The acceptance of "we're fine, we have the risks covered by credit default swaps" proved to be the undoing of a number of companies who had committed to, or dabbled in, credit derivatives, just as the acceptance of asset-backed commercial paper as being "as safe as a money market account" proved unwise by others. All of this points to a level of complexity that may not match our capacity to either analyze or manage.

A third hypothesis is that we don't really expose developing talent in our organizations to a comprehensive understanding of risk as they progress through their careers. To the extent that they serve in marketing roles they get exposure to brand risk; in treasury roles they get to understand market risk; in IT or manufacturing roles they are exposed to operational risk and so on. But these exposures are seldom planned or systematic. Do we need to change our thinking on this so that executives of the future approach their senior roles with a better, holistic and comprehensive understanding of risk and its origins, mitigation and management? How would we build these exposures into programs and developmental experiences so that we developed ·a new generation of leaders who understood risk better, not so that they could avoid risk but so that they could make better decisions and more effectively monitor the consequences of those decisions?

Systems Complexity

Many analysts of the financial and economic crisis suggest that leaders at the top of organizations lost touch with what was really going on because the system itself had become so complex that no one in a leadership role could ever really understand how it worked. Even if they knew what was going on, they may have had difficulty putting their finger either on which risks they failed to account for or on what part of their oversight failed. For example, the "chain" linking writing a sub-prime mortgage in Philadelphia and AIG defaulting on a credit default swap was so complex that even leaders in senior roles did not understand the consequences of a downturn in the property market for the health of the whole financial system. That these smart, bright people appeared stunned in trying to explain what happened and why was rooted in the sheer complexity of the system that they had created. The "machine" developed by humans had become a "system" that defied human understanding, and the inability to understand it created a sense of detachment from it and, therefore, a minimization of personal culpability for things that went wrong.

This is also the case in the broader economy. For the sake of efficiency, firms are becoming more specialized on core, value-added, distinctive competencies and are outsourcing everything else. So, for example, the car companies have become marketers and final assemblers and rely on first, second, third and fourth tier suppliers. Food processing companies make the final product but depend on ingredients that are sourced from many different parts of the world. Mattel, the toy and games company, ran into a problem because a supplier to a supplier to a supplier to a supplier to Mattel used lead-based paint that was outside Mattel's specifications.

As these chains get longer and more complicated they get harder to manage, and the models we use to guide managers have not been developed or studied in these increasingly complicated environments. This leads to unintended consequences where miscreants, cheats or the merely negligent are not detected but only found out when their defects are incorporated into the final products and services and show up as consequences for customers, clients, public health, brand damage and so on.

Complex systems are the breeding ground for disasters[11] and the implications of this "systems complexity" hypothesis for leadership development are profound. From a strategic standpoint, many leaders and managers are pursuing efficiency through outsourcing or networking to lower their costs while at the same time taking on, and not accounting for, the increased risk of this activity. Consider that a fatal flaw in one part of the system has the potential for total failure of the entire system when they are interconnected but with no redundancy. From an organizational standpoint, the conventional models of management based on transaction cost and agency theories[12] are simply inadequate for this vastly more complex environment.

We need to expose leaders and those with leadership potential to systems-thinking while also paying more serious attention

11 A compelling example of this is Snook's analysis of the accidental shooting down of two Black Hawk helicopters by friendly F-15s over Northern Iraq in April 1991. There were all sorts of safeguards to ensure this type of tragic event would not happen, yet Snook's account reveals that "this accident happened because of, or perhaps in spite of, everyone behaving just the way we would expect them to behave, just the way theory would predict – given a clear understanding of the circumstances. Indeed, this accident was 'normal'...because it occurred as a result of normal people behaving in normal ways in normal organizations." For a detailed analysis see *Friendly Fire* by Scott Snook, (New Jersey: Princeton University Press, 2000), 202.

12 Transaction Cost Economics (Williamson, 1981; Coase, 1937) focuses on the costs a firm incurs by exchanging with external agents. These costs can be broken down into production costs (the cost of turning inputs into outputs) and transaction costs (the costs of exchanging with external agents). As long as the lower production costs from outsourcing come with sufficiently low transaction costs, outsourcing is the way to go. However, as systems become more complex, transaction costs increase, primarily because it is hard to ensure that agents act in the firm's best interest. Agency Theory (Jensen and Meckling, 1976) covers similar ground to Transaction Cost Economics by focusing on creating contracts that will ensure that the incentives of the agent are aligned with the company.

Coase, R. (1937). "The Nature of the Firm." *Economica* 4 (16): 386–405.

Jensen, M., and Meckling, W. (1976). "Theory of the firm: Managerial behavior, agency costs, and ownership structure." *Journal of Financial Economics*, 3: 305–360.

Williamson, Oliver E. (1981). "The Economics of Organization: The Transaction Cost Approach." *The American Journal of Sociology*, 87(3): 548–577.

to the perspectives that enable us to more clearly understand the behavioral implications of the systems we are building. These systems demand the skills of leading and managing people who don't report to you or even to your organizations, and values-based leadership that extends beyond the organization to the supply chains and networks on which they are dependent.

There are real impediments to offering this type of education and development. An overwhelming drive for greater simplicity in concepts, for shorter formal programs, for books that lay out "silver bullets," all fight against the need to get people immersed in understanding and coming to grips with system complexity. How can we persuade people that such immersion will be beneficial and worth the effort?

Leadership Psychology

There are many who believe that the primary cause of both the overheated, credit-hungry boom followed by the recession and financial crisis had more to do with psychology rather than fundamental economics, although with the modern thinking about behavioral economics, theories of rational expectations and so on, such distinctions may be moot. Many analyses focus on four distinct psychological constructs: overconfidence, hubris, groupthink and social conformity.

Many of history's great tragedies have stemmed from the overconfidence of leaders.[13] The dash of the Titanic through the North Atlantic ice fields, Napoleon's march on Moscow, the allied armies' invasion of Gallipoli, the Bay of Pigs debacle and even the pursuit of the Hebrews by Pharaoh's armies are all examples in which individual leaders' self-confidence became

13 M. Gladwell, "Cocksure: Banks, Battles and the Psychology of Over-Confidence," The New Yorker, July 27, 2009.

exaggerated. Overconfidence is not only common among certain types of leaders in certain occupations, but it has been described as an essential adaptive trait that may be required to be successful in certain kinds of businesses.[14]

With repeated episodes of "winning" comes a belief that winning is an entitlement and that losing is not possible. At this stage, overconfidence has become hubris, and when executives have high hubris it can have a negative impact on the strategic decision-making process, the actual strategic choices that are made and ultimately organizational performance.[15] Perennial winners cloak themselves in a mantle of righteous armor that is impervious to criticism, self-doubt or pleas to exercise caution. Like Icarus of Greek mythology, they soar higher and higher until they fly too close to the sun and discover that they are, indeed, only mortals who perish when their wings melt in the extreme heat.

In the years 1993–2008, with a blip in 2001–2002, we were living in a growing economy, albeit one fueled by increased personal indebtedness. So many in the financial services industry, especially in investment banking, got so used to success that they could not envisage failure. These "masters of the universe," celebrated and then ridiculed by novelist Tom Wolfe in *The Bonfire of the Vanities*, felt invulnerable, superhuman and beyond the reach of even the most fundamental laws of economics. Their schemes for making money became more and more audacious; sub-prime mortgages morphed into highly leveraged collateralized debt obligations (CDOs); derivatives of these became CDOs-squared with multiples of that leverage. The party was going on forever and the piper never had

---

14 R. Wrangham, "Is Military Incompetence Adaptive?" *Evolution and Human Behavior* 20(1) (1999), 3–17

15 N.J. Hiller and D.C. Hambrick, "Conceptualizing Executive Hubris: The Role of (Hyper-) Core Self-Evaluations in Strategic Decision Making," *Strategic Management Journal* 26 (2005): 297–319.

to be paid—or so they thought. One after another, investment bankers appeared in front of Congressman Henry Waxman's Committee on Oversight and Government Reform in October 2008 and proclaimed that "they never saw it coming," or words to that effect.

Whereas individuals display hubris, successful, highly cohesive groups exhibit groupthink, a kind of collective hubris described by sociologist and journalist William H. Whyte and researched by Irving Janis[16] and others. Such groups tend to develop the illusion that they are invulnerable and unanimous in their thinking and a deep belief that their actions are moral. Naturally, these beliefs make them feel that nothing bad can happen to them. These illusions blind them to the warning signs of potential danger and desensitize them to anyone within or outside the group who might raise concerns about group decisions or actions. They stereotype, denigrate and demonize anyone inside or outside their immediate circle who may think that what they are doing is ill conceived or just plain wrong. They prevent those with dissenting views from gaining access to key decision-makers. It leads to a collective overconfidence that denies reality. There was a chilling interview with a senior executive at Lehman Brothers who said, in describing how the company's mortgage business grew rapidly as it led a deterioration in credit requirements to get a mortgage, "When you're at a party, a good party, there are times when you just don't want to leave."

There were many who warned of the grave dangers of being courted by those building financial houses of cards on the top of a financial bubble, from Nobel Prize-winning economists to former policy makers. There were people inside banks who

16 Irving L. Janis, *Victims of Groupthink* (Boston: Houghton Mifflin Company, 1972), 9; William H. Whyte (1952) *Fortune.*

sounded cautionary alarms but whose views were rejected as non-entrepreneurial or too risk-averse. There were e-mails and text messages flying around the rating agencies that stated, frankly, that much of this financial engineering was a chimera.

But the disease of groupthink acts to repel critics, to shut out dissenters, to marginalize those who are critical of the way things are done by the "winning" team. It has been linked to the Bay of Pigs debacle in the Kennedy administration, to the failures that NASA experienced with the *Challenger* and *Columbia* space shuttles and to other apparently "stupid" actions by "smart" people. It should come as no surprise to see it at work in many heretofore-successful financial companies as well as in other "too big to fail" companies such as General Motors.

Groupthink arises not just at the organization level but at the sector level as well. When everyone else is doing it, as in the case of structured products (or outsourcing more generally), you have to do it as well, otherwise you are deemed to be failing—you will underperform your peers. Although Canadian banks did not engage they were frequently targeted as being underperformers on the global stage. The hammer here is that taking on these risks and doing equally well on the upside is necessary, and losing while your peers are losing is not viewed badly. Very few people applauded underperformance when firms stayed out of the structured products market, even when they knew it was risky. Goldman Sachs did not stay out of the market, they just bought insurance to cover it in case it did explode. In Canada, Moody's and S&P would not rate Canadian asset-backed commercial paper because of the risks. DBRS did rate it and people bought it like crazy.

Finally, there is the problem of social conformity—a desire to go along with those whom you like and respect even if you believe that they are wrong in their actions. It is this subconscious desire to conform, the dislike of rocking the boat, that leads people to ignore wrongdoing or accept inaction in the face of events that call for action to be taken.

What is frustrating is that the dangers of overconfidence, hubris, groupthink and conformity have been high on the agendas of all management and executive development programs at business schools and in-company universities and leadership academies for decades. We actually know quite a lot about these social-psychological constructs. However, there is a gap between recognizing a phenomenon intellectually and accepting that it can happen to us! Furthermore, we often fail to accept responsibility for the cultures that we help to create that allow these phenomena to play themselves out in the ways in which decisions are made in our organizations.[17]

These are not new realizations. Yet we continue to see egotistical executives, who may publicly embrace Collins' Level 5 leadership trait of "fierce humility" yet be so lacking in it themselves, emerging in top positions in very important companies. Why is it that decisions to promote these people, or ratify their promotions, are being made day in and day out? What is it that top managements and boards see in these people that doesn't scream "Danger!"?

There are many implications for leadership and leadership development arising from these sets of issues. Organizations must put in place systems (and provide adequate resources for their maintenance) that allow for proper "scanning" of the environment and—perhaps more important—the integration of information or signals that might help people conclude a

17 Philip Zimbardo, *The Lucifer Effect: Understanding How Good People Turn Evil* (New York: Random House, 2005). Philip Zimbardo provides a chilling account, using the Stanford Prison Experiment, abuses at the Abu Ghraib prison and much other research to reveal why "good people do bad things." He helps to discount the notion of bad apples and reveals that bad barrels and bad barrel-makers are critical. Yet no player in "the system" would see their own wrongdoing.

predictable surprise is "around the corner." Moreover, they must expose developing leaders to these activities so that they, too, can develop an understanding of the "bigger picture." A greater emphasis on "what-if" analysis, rigorous debriefing of the outcomes of decisions and challenging assumptions all would help developing leaders hone their rational decision-making skills.

We recognize that there are organizations that value this type of decision-making and others for whom it is anathema— too "theoretical" or "academic." The "learning" organizations have a culture of analysis, learning from actions and using learning loops to improve their decisions. The others value swift action above all else and tend to associate careful analysis with lack of decisiveness. In addition to making rational, fact-based decision-making easier to understand and practice, what we need to do as educators and leadership developers is demonstrate that there is a positive payback to developing this form of organizational culture and a negative consequence of not doing so.

Executive Compensation

We have always recognized the need to align executive and managerial compensation with the interests of shareholders by incentivizing behaviors that serve shareholders' interests and rewarding the results. Yet it is obvious from the events of the last few years that something has gone very wrong with this alignment. There is little doubt that compensation systems played a major role in causing some of the problems in the economic/financial crash, and we are now painfully aware that many of these compensation systems failed to take into full account the longer-term risk that was associated with leveraging firms to achieve short-term results.

Nowhere is this truer than in the asset-gathering, deal-making and financial-engineering parts of the financial services businesses. Mortgage brokers, most investment advisers and many financial advisers and consultants—those who gather assets from retail investors—make most of their money from compensation pools created by that asset gathering and not on the performance of those assets after they have been gathered. The securitizers make their money when they bundle these assets and sell them to others, not on how those securities perform. The deal-makers make their money from fees based on the money they raise to do a deal and not on what happens to the buyer/seller stocks after the deal is done. And the financial engineers make their money by increasing leverage.

What is true is that almost all executive level players in publicly traded companies have some alignment between their personal wealth and the long-term success of their employers and other stockholders in their companies. They hold substantial amounts of stock units, deferred stock and stock options that will only pay off if there is performance of the stock over mid to long terms. Clearly, when Bear Stearns went under and Lehman collapsed, Jimmy Cayne and Dick Fuld lost considerable amounts of their wealth as their stock values collapsed. But these were very wealthy men with diversified holdings. They did not, like many pension and retirement fund holders, have all of their eggs in one basket. There is a major difference between an already wealthy person having a paper profit from a stock option that's in the money disappear, and a modest income earner actually losing 40 percent of the value of their IRA, 401K or RRSP, and to suggest that there is alignment through such compensation schemes is naïve.

It also is clear that compensation systems often have been designed to incentivize and reward performance by individuals and teams to the detriment of the rest of their organizations. The story of AIG is classic; here, a very small group of people, those in the financial products (that is, derivatives) business, perhaps no more than 100 in all, jeopardized the financial integrity of the whole corporation by betting the shop to build a large, lucrative but incredibly risky business that required pledging of the whole of the firm's capital base and more.[18] When this business blew up, the whole company almost went with it, and it was only a massive infusion of capital by the federal government so that it could satisfy the counter-party risks it had taken on through derivatives contracts that kept the "good" parts of the company (an excellent insurance business) alive.

One concern is that the emphasis in the design of executive compensation systems of many companies that ran into trouble was firmly on attracting and retaining "top talent." This is also the concern that those who run these companies today are expressing as they fight governments' attempts to control compensation practices. That this is an extremely self-serving position is not lost on them and, at least behind the scenes, there is much discussion about making executive compensation more risk-related as well as reflective of the investment that has been made in these companies by the taxpayer.

It seems obvious that we must take the whole topic of executive compensation from being the purview of consultants and compensation committees of boards and make it a mainstream issue for boards and management teams in organizations. It is not a "personnel" or "human resources" concern but, rather, a central issue in risk management. It should be taught under that rubric in business schools and should be addressed by risk management committees of boards, senior managements of companies and others responsible for risk management.

---

18 M. Lewis, "The Man Who Crashed the World," *Vanity Fair*, August 2009.

Directorial Delinquency

Joining the issues of long-term outlook, risk, system complexity and executive compensation reveals deep flaws in a system for which no one seems to be accountable. Where was corporate governance in this mess? "How," people ask, "could the management of firms such as Merrill Lynch, Bear Stearns, UBS, AIG and many, many others be allowed to bet their firms in the ways they did? Where was the oversight, the governance that should have prevented this from happening?"

It has become increasingly clear that many of the firms that got themselves into trouble were run by CEOs who were legends in their industries and, some would say, in their own minds, who would brook no opposition or criticism of their actions by anyone, including their hand-picked boards of directors.

Outsized executive egos, overconfidence, hubris and group-think should not shock experienced corporate directors. These issues have been around as long as there have been entrepreneurs and organized corporations. Nor should directors be naïve enough to believe that managers act solely in the interests of shareholders—that becomes obvious in most discussions over executive appointments, bonuses, change of control agreements and other elements of executive compensation. Yet it appears, on the surface, that many directors were either complicit with management, simply naïve about what was going on in many of the organizations at the epicenter of the financial crisis, or unwilling to make waves in the boardroom by challenging the actions of management or the past decisions of directors to engage in risky business.

It may take a long time and much research of a very difficult type to really answer the question of "where were the directors?" However, there are some plausible hypotheses that might explain yet another failure of governance. Many directors joined the boards of financial institutions in the days when life was a lot simpler. It was not hard to understand such things as minimum capital requirements, capital tiers, non-performing loans and so on. When CDOs, structured investment vehicles, credit default swaps and other derivative products came along, it was easy to feign an understanding of these risk management vehicles. It also was hard for directors to speak up and say, "Stop! I don't understand these things" and resist their adoption until they did understand them. So they got used to accepting such practices mutely, to not recognizing the risks that were being taken, to rewarding senior executives handsomely for short-run returns, to comforting themselves that since much of this reward was in the form of stock or stock options, the interests of management and shareholders were compatible. When the houses of cards started to collapse it was extraordinarily difficult for such directors to demand explanations of schemes that they had so blithely and recently approved and which, by then, had reached such huge levels of complexity that even those who had spent their whole lives in risk management had difficulty understanding. And, by the time the actions of management became fully known, it was too late.

A second hypothesis is that boards were content to have one or two directors who truly did understand the risks that were being taken act on behalf of the board, either as a risk management committee or as director-monitors. If these "expert" directors were industry insiders, their perspectives and susceptibility to the forces described above were likely to be those of their respective senior management teams, especially if they had been selected and in effect served at the pleasure of those managers. Hence, they were either unable or unwilling to guide the boards in their oversight responsibilities. The very existence of these so-called expert directors may have led to non-expert directors abdicating their governance role.

Finally, for all of its good intentions and for all of its "independence," a board is subject to the same influences, including social conformity and groupthink, as other groups. After years of delivering outstanding results to shareholders, it is understandable that a board might resist questioning or even challenging managers who were pursuing the very strategies that had brought so much past success. While this may be understandable, it is not acceptable.

The Enron and WorldCom scandals, together with Sarbanes-Oxley–driven legislation, focused attention on corporate governance, and there is no shortage of programs and courses on corporate governance or consultants prepared to offer such education to intact boards. A cursory examination of who attends these programs suggests that novice directors or those who aspire to become directors view them as necessary. Yet the directorial delinquency that characterized the financial and economic crisis of 2007–2009 was evidenced by highly experienced directors rather than novices.

It is tempting to think that the events of the last couple of years may have raised the consciousness of directors to systemic and organizational risk and that they would be more likely to seek or accept higher levels of education about risk, systems thinking, complex systems and executive compensation than they appear to have sought in the past. But it begs the question: "What can we, as educators and leadership developers, do to make such education more accessible, more acceptable and more relevant for experienced directors and more attractive for intact boards to schedule as part of their ongoing calendars of activities?"

Competencies and Character

In recent years, organizations have become obsessed with identifying the competencies that they require in their leaders and, consequently, leadership development activities have become focused on increasing those competencies. Obviously, competencies are important and we have referred to many of these—environmental scanning, rational decision-making, analyzing complex systems—in this book. But while competencies determine what a leader can do, what he or she will do in a situation is determined much more by their character.

At times like this it is useful to recall Aristotle's description of some of the key components of the moral character.[19] In addition to the requirements for honesty, integrity and others, they include courage, which allows managers to assume reasonable risks demonstrating initiative without being foolhardy and speaking up when they believe something is wrong; temperance, which allows managers to channel their drives and ambitions in creative and useful ways that avoid excesses; and justice, which is the virtue associated with trying to find fitting balances between competing forces and is essential to considering and balancing stakeholder claims. Character, according to Aristotle, is formed through living, reflecting on how one lives, receiving feedback and criticism and refining one's approach to living.

Leadership development must address both competencies and character development, but we suspect that the latter receives short shrift in both business schools and corporate learning development programs. There are many reasons for this, including some reluctance to address "character" because it is a personal matter, some lack of skills in formulating and

---

19 Aristotle discusses his approach to moral living in *Nicomachean Ethics*.

addressing character issues and some concern that "teaching" can become "preaching" when it comes to character issues. Despite these reasons, it is essential that we persist in developing useful and acceptable ways of addressing the character issues both in programs and in the way we coach and mentor individuals in leadership roles. When companies develop formal leadership profiles that address these character elements, this provides an impetus for such education and development efforts.

Conclusion

A long-held view of the relationship between business and society is that within democratic capitalist systems, business has a conditional license to operate. It will be free to do so provided it serves the expressed and implicit needs of the societies within which it operates. When it ceases to do so, its freedoms will be curbed[20] either by regulatory action or by the behaviors of customers in the marketplace.

In our view, the shortcomings of business leadership that have been exposed during the recent financial and economic crisis have come very close to undermining the legitimacy of the capitalist system and it is almost inevitable that regulations will be tightened; that calls for greater consumer protection to be endorsed by politicians and regulators.

It will take years for the real cause and effect analyses of this financial meltdown and economic crisis to be completed and, even then, there will be questions about who did what and why. But we cannot wait for years—the world moves too quickly.

We need to take to heart philosopher Santayana's oft-misquoted warning: "Those who do not learn from history

---

20 This formulation of the social responsibility of business was provided in a 1982 personal communication from David Grier, a long-time public relations executive with Royal Bank Group.

are doomed to repeat it."[21] Lessons have been—indeed are being—learned from this mess but it is not a given that these lessons will stick. Asset bubbles have come and gone in the past; the dot.com era that spawned the insane rise in the NASDAQ, the Asian property asset value collapse and long-term capital management are recent rather than ancient history.

Will the excesses of the last few years be repeated, or will leaders of the future have a smarter approach to regulation, better governance, better risk management and better leadership in our organizations?

Even today, those who run investment banks and trading houses justify the need to return to high-risk compensation practices that were identified as part of the problem because of the competitive system that has bid up the price of these "masters of the universe." The damaged institutions that relied on money from the Troubled Asset Relief Program to bail them out are repaying this money early so that they can escape the supervision of the Obama administration's pay czar and get back to the old ways of doing things. The Financial Services Authority in the U.K. is backpedaling furiously on its proposals to dramatically increase oversight of non-bank financial institutions for fear of destroying the City of London's preeminence as a financial center.

Toughening of legislation in many parts of the world is being resisted by those who believe that "freer is better," either as an ideological mantra or on the basis of well-considered and thoughtful balancing of pros and cons of free-market and tightly regulated financial systems. As we write this chapter the global stock markets have recovered half of their losses from their

---

21 Santayana's actual words were, "Those who cannot remember the past are condemned to repeat it" but the usual misquotation is used above.

lows in March 2009[22] and economic "green shoots" are being heralded as a harbinger of a new period of slow but sustainable economic growth. There is evidence that people are "bored with bad news" and want to focus on the positives. The financial and economic crisis of 2007–2009 gave way to a period of recovery before its impact on public finances plunged the world into the sovereign debt crisis of 2010. Now, in mid-2010, even the most optimistic scenarios talk of years of rebuilding public finances, reduction of household debt and recapitalization of the world's financial system before anything like historical trend-line economic growth returns in developed countries. There will be wrenching adjustments for many countries in the Euro area, and it is not yet certain that the eurozone is viable.

In a Bloomberg.com posting on September 12, 2009, the authors note: One year after the demise of Lehman Brothers Holdings Inc. paralyzed the financial system, "mega-banks,"… are as interconnected and inscrutable as ever. The Obama administration's plan for a regulatory overhaul wouldn't force them to shrink or simplify their structure.

"We could have another Lehman Monday," Niall Ferguson, author of the 2008 book *The Ascent of Money* and a professor of history at Harvard University in Cambridge, Massachusetts, said in an interview. "The system is essentially unchanged, except that post-Lehman, the survivors have 'too big to fail' tattooed on their chests."[23]

In this chapter we have suggested a number of things that we should be doing to extract and apply the learning from this recent experience so that leadership will be improved:

---

22 The Dow Jones Industrial Average hit a low of 6,547 on March 9, 2009.
23 Alison Fitzgerald and Christine Harper, "Lehman Monday Morning Lesson Lost with Obama Regulator-in-Chief," Bloomberg.com, September 11, 2009, http://www.bloomberg.com/apps/news?pid=20601109&sid=aUTh4YMml6QE

- We need to ensure that leaders of the future learn from the past, and that means a greater exposure to economic history and a sensitization to the social consequences of poor business leadership.
- We need to create a greater capability to scan the economic, political, societal and technological environments to identify those "predictable crises" before they emerge in full-blown form.
- We need to help people recognize the social-psychological processes at work that distort reality and interfere with rational decision-making.
- We must increase the self-awareness of leaders so that they are alert to the problems that they may be having with such processes and so that they can avoid creating organizational cultures in which overconfidence, hubris, groupthink and conformity are commonplace.
- We need to improve corporate governance practices, especially with respect to the selection of leaders who are less egocentric than many who occupy leadership roles today.
- We need to improve leaders' understanding of complex systems and how to analyze the consequences of action and inaction on organizations and individuals within those systems.
- We need to elevate discussions about executive compensation from a human resources issue to a fundamental consideration in risk management.
- We need to focus as much on the character of leaders, and the development of that character in next generation leaders, as we focus on their competencies.
- We need to instill in next generation leaders a deeper sense of responsibility, not just to their personal wealth or

shareholder wealth, but to the health of the systems and societies in which they operate.

Finally, we look forward to engaging you in dialog and discussion about the analysis, thoughts and conclusions represented in this paper. We know that you have a stake, as we do, in developing our leaders of the future and hope that you will share these with us in the weeks ahead.

* * *

The implications arising from the "leadership on trial" initiative for cross-enterprise leadership are significant. The analysis of the issues that led to the crises and the initial insights arising from the analysis point to the importance of cross-enterprise leadership. It was clear that problems arose because of the failure of leaders to understand the cross-enterprise nature of the systems in which they operated, whether that be the context of complexity and ambiguity or the risks that were embedded and unidentified across the enterprise and across enterprises. As well, it was clear that many leaders did not possess the character or competencies of the cross-enterprise leader. The global economic crisis has served as a real-time case study on the need for cross-enterprise leadership.

As for the future, we do not accept the inevitability that the excesses, misjudgments and negligence of the last few years must somehow be repeated, but we recognize that they could. It will require better leadership at the top of organizations, improved education and development of leaders today and among the next generations of leaders, better regulators, and policy makers and politicians who are able to climb above immediate electoral concerns and take the long view. Cynics would say this will never happen; skeptics say that it's unlikely; we say there is no alternative.

~Conclusion~

Cross-Enterprise Leadership: The Way Forward

by Mary Crossan

In chapter 1 we described cross-enterprise leadership as a holistic approach to value creation in the enterprise. It recognizes four emergent realities that redefine general management for the challenges of the 21st-century manager. First, whereas general management focused on integrating the various functions within an organization, the business imperative today requires an approach—cross-enterprise leadership—that can create, capture and distribute value across a network of companies, not just within a company. Second, these networks, which we call enterprises, are complex and dynamic and must be able to respond as a whole to the emergent challenges that are continually presented. Third, no one leader can "manage" the enterprise, and therefore leadership needs to be distributed.

Finally, these changes require an approach to leadership over and above that possessed by traditional business leaders. At its core, cross-enterprise leadership recognizes that managers operate within a complex world where the boundaries of organizations are fluid and dynamic, cutting across functional designations, departments, business units, companies, geography and cultures.

The compelling need for cross-enterprise leadership became painfully apparent as global economies faltered like a house of cards, a situation precipitated largely by events in the United States. Organizations and economies are interconnected at a level unprecedented in history. This interconnection is by design in the case of global supply chain networks, and in the case of political regulations enable the free flow of trade and assets, but it has also emerged in ways that are less apparent, largely through the instantaneous and low-cost interconnectivity offered through technology. That goods and services are delivered through interconnected systems, as opposed to singular organizations, speaks to the need for leadership cross-enterprise.

Yet cross-enterprise leadership is more than leadership across organizations. It stems from the capacity of organizations to muster their full potential by ensuring they reap the benefits of innovation and execution that do not know the bounds of functions, business units or geography. Whether private or public sector, for profit or not for profit, small or large, organizations of all types seek more efficient and effective ways to deliver products and services, calling for cross-enterprise leadership of their own organizations.

We described the role of the cross-enterprise leader in chapter 2, emphasizing the importance of five core actions:

1. Understand and interpret the environment in which you operate.
2. Develop winning strategies.
3. Execute them brilliantly.
4. Measure the impact of your strategies systematically, adjusting strategies as indicated.
5. Develop organizational, departmental, team and personal capabilities.

As described in chapter 2, this outward- and forward-looking requirement cannot be delegated to a small set of specialized scenario-creators or confined to a few days or weeks of the year. The chief financial officer must scan the financial environment; the head of human resources must be alert to changes in labor markets and legislation that affects the workforce; the chief information officer must recognize developments in information technology that could create or destroy competitive advantage. Looking at the developing environment isn't just required of senior executives: The credit manger must look at rising consumer debt levels, the purchasing manager must think of commodity price movements and the things that influence them, the facilities manager must decide whether to go long or short on energy prices . . . and so on. Leadership at *all* levels must be focused on the future as well as the present.

Someone, at any level of leadership, who is tasked with the responsibility of seeing issues, analyzing them and acting with the interests and perspectives of the total enterprise, we described as the "secret sauce" of the cross-enterprise leader in chapter 3. They have four types of specific intelligence: strategic, business, people and organizational. By "intelligence" we mean knowledge, understanding of key concepts and relationships between variables, and skills in these four critical areas of executive competence. These must be underpinned by a reasonably high general intellect, the fifth type of intelligence. Cross-enterprise leadership capability knits these intelligences together and requires a set of character strengths and virtues, the importance of which were highlighted in chapter 10, where we described an initiative that engaged leaders in forums that enabled us to learn from the economic crisis by considering what needs to be done to develop the next generation of leaders. The importance of character loomed large, not just in a sense of ethical decision-making, but as a set of traits that are fundamental to how leaders analyze and make decisions. These traits are also at the core of whether and how deeply leaders develop the other intelligences. Borrowing from the work of Peterson and Seligman, we described these character strengths and virtues as follows:

- **Wisdom**—Creativity, curiosity, open-mindedness, love of learning and perspective are critical to deepening and developing one's leadership capability. A key aspect of this learning capability is dealing with complexity and ambiguity. As one executive described it, "It is okay to get caught in the headlights, but it is not okay to be frozen in them."

- **Temperateness**—Being temperate involves curbing the tendency to excess, which entails having modesty, self-control and humility. The leader who thinks he or she knows everything is not in a very good position to learn. Furthermore, learning often arises from making mistakes, and many people do not want to admit mistakes to themselves or others. Many leaders fall short in this area since they assume that being a leader means they have all the answers.

- **Integrity**—Having an ethical worldview that you can articulate and rely on to wade through the messy and challenging leadership issues is essential. We have encountered many leaders who have no moral compass and who tend to lose their way as a result. Peterson and Seligman referred to this as a sense of "justice." It is the preparedness as a leader "to do the right thing in the right way" all of the time and to be a coherent, authentic person both in one's persona as a formal organizational leader and as a private individual. The leader with integrity does not abandon that when he or she walks into the office, no matter how tempting it is to take the most expedient approach that leads away from the ethical path.

- **Compassion**—Often lost in discussions of leadership is the deep connection to those one leads. Peterson and Seligman refer to this as a sense of humanity, and some of the most powerful forms of leadership have roots in humanity. We interpret it as respect for those one leads and passion for the cause that is grounded in this respect.

- **Courage**—What we see lacking in many leaders is a "fire in their belly" that is required to lead. Passion and courage are not abstract concepts but rather real manifestations of why an individual wants to lead and what he or she hopes to accomplish. Courage also acknowledges that leaders face extremely challenging situations in pursuit of their aims. Having persistence and vitality to face obstacles is critical.

- **Transcendence**—Often, achieving greatness requires having a level of aspiration that transcends the obvious. It is a rather rare and interesting collection of character strengths,

in the form of hope, humor, gratitude, a sense of spirituality and appreciation of excellence, that appear to foster the
capacity to transcend. The challenge for leaders in many
organizations is to appreciate the place for this kind of
transcendence. However, apart from religious leaders, like
the Dalai Lama, who embody this quality, many leaders
find the grind of the daily leadership challenge drives out
any possibility of transcendence.

When these six virtues are accompanied by the five "intelligences," they form the knowledge, understanding, skill, judgment and character required to be a cross-enterprise leader.
In chapter 6 we described how we at Ivey develop the cross-
enterprise leader. While business schools such as ours help to
fill the gap in developing the cross-enterprise leader, it is not
enough. Leadership development within organizations is essential and needs to go beyond what is often a typical focus on
"leading people" to embrace the broader set of intelligences and
capabilities we have described. Yet there is also a responsibility
for individuals to take ownership for their own development.
You can read about what it takes to become a cross-enterprise
leader, however learning and development occurs when you
put these ideas into action then reflect on the experience and
deepen your leadership capability as a result.

We are grateful to Bill Aziz for his interview, which helps to
unpack the ideas of cross-enterprise leadership as we consider
them in the context of turnaround management. In chapter 4
he reminds us that cross-enterprise leadership is not some lofty
perspective when he observes:

I think that cross-enterprise leaders are, by nature, people who need to understand how things work at a very granular level. Leaders can't lead across an enterprise without understanding what goes on in the enterprise. When I served on a board in the United States, the CEO used to call me the "Why Why Guy" because on significant issues I kept drilling to understand more. People who drill into the functions in the organization can then use their skills and knowledge to understand how a decision in one area might impact another. If your style is collaborative and you have a good management team, you lead or influence others to think that way, too. The cross-enterprise leader is someone who fundamentally wants to understand how a business works and why. That can lead to re-thinking and tearing down many things that are done just because they've been done that way for a long time.

We also applied cross-enterprise leadership to entrepreneurial contexts, engaging emerging markets and building sustainable value. That effective entrepreneurs embody the spirit of cross-enterprise leadership was evidenced in chapter 5. In addition to being responsible for the operation of the entire business, entrepreneurs face ambiguous situations, uncertain futures and scarce resources with which to address these situations. The environment is often complex and dynamic, typically with an abundance of stakeholders and internal and external networks, resulting in fuzzy organizational boundaries. Yet, despite what seems like insurmountable challenges, many entrepreneurs succeed in building companies that go on to drive growth in the economy. Successful entrepreneurs are able to look at the holistic picture of the enterprise, no matter its size, and see where connections can be made with employees, customers and partners.

In chapter 7 we applied cross-enterprise leadership to research on engaging the Chinese market and emerging markets more generally. The development of a China strategy, let alone a strategy for all emerging markets, is a major challenge for any leader—in fact, the list of challenges may occasionally seem to be insurmountable. However, many of the reasons we heard for avoiding doing business with China were anchored in old-fashioned functional "silo-thinking," rather than focused on how thinking cross-enterprise might help firms tackle core business issues successfully. We described practical approaches for the cross-enterprise leader. The first step in developing strategic intelligence with regard to a China strategy is to simply get out from behind the desk and go to China to begin reducing the uncertainty around the go/no go decision and to fully assess the risk/return trade-offs. Business intelligence can be honed through further training and development or job rotation programs that stretch leaders out of their comfortable areas of expertise. Organizational intelligence requires a candid examination of the structures, systems, procedures and policies within the firm that might be contributing to an organizational culture resistant to a China strategy, while developing people intelligence is anchored in a commitment to listen, learn, understand and motivate individuals to achieve extraordinary results. All four intelligences, as well as a certain degree of general intellect, are the basic ingredients of cross-enterprise leadership capability. The leadership challenge for those executives tasked with developing and executing a China strategy is to honestly diagnose their strengths and weaknesses in each area and commit to developing the skills required to lead cross-enterprise.

In chapter 8 we tackled head on the question: Should corporate managers be required to be socially responsible, or should they confine themselves solely to pursuing shareholder value by all legal means? This question is at the heart of many cross-enterprise leadership challenges as leaders consider whose interests they are serving. The chapter examines this question from a historical perspective and distills a simple fact of life: *Businesses have a conditional license to operate.* To the extent that they meet the expectations of society, they will be encouraged and allowed to operate freely. When they violate those expectations they will be regulated, controlled or even prevented from doing business, either by the behaviors of people in the marketplace or by governments and their agencies. While caring for society is a noble and worthy virtue in and of itself, it is also an act of enlightened self-interest. This view differs from "greed" in that it recognizes self-interest and the interests of others in society and it seeks to maximize self-interest subject to the consequences for others. Its moral foundation rests on recognizing, integrating or balancing legitimate interests, whereas greed is the pursuit of self-interest in ignorance of, or despite, the interests or needs of others.

Much of the debate about the social responsibility of business has focused on large corporations, at least to date. However, more and more the owners and operators of small and medium-size businesses are being called to account for their impact on their communities and environments. Cross-enterprise leaders must have a deep understanding of the case for and against businesses taking societal preferences and impact into consideration when making decisions. To constructively engage the critics and the supporters of business, they must consider the case for business social responsibility as both a moral imperative and a sensible business decision in the interests of shareholders. Business leaders must identify the potential areas of interest that CSR may have in their organizations and where there may be friction. This may involve reviewing product formulations, packaging, distribution processes, supply chain relationships, community involvement and many, many other areas. This is not a trivial exercise. More and more CSR groups have become expert at analyzing the social performance of business, detecting superficial responses to their concerns and exposing insincere attempts to address real issues.

The mission statement of the Richard Ivey School of Business is "To develop business leaders who think globally, act strategically and contribute to the societies within which they operate." There is nothing soft or sentimental about this statement. It reflects the reality that business enterprises live in symbiotic relationships with the societies in which they operate and have a vested interest in ensuring the health of those societies. Whether awareness of social issues and pro-social actions is driven by moral conviction or crass financial interest is moot. Failing to recognize the role of business in society and take a stance on key social issues will almost certainly lead to poor analysis of business situations and poor decision-making. Good decision-making in today's business environment depends on leaders who are committed to driving shareholder value, sensitized to social issues and trends and who are creative in positioning their organizations on the right side of the issues. The future of the capitalist system, which, for all its flaws, has delivered great benefits and is the hope for the developing world, may depend on it.

The compelling case for cross-enterprise leadership to build sustainable value was made in chapter 9. Businesses can be agents of positive change instead of the target of public criticism when they take actions that meet the needs of the present without compromising future generations to meet their own needs. Doing so requires them to consider how their decisions and actions contribute to the principles of economic efficiency, social equity and environmental integrity. We offered several mechanisms through which to make this happen: by expanding the dimension of firm performance; by looking beyond boundaries and integrating knowledge from diverse perspectives; by appreciating the dynamic and complex environment; and by building distributed, empowered and dynamic leadership. The Network for Business Sustainability is one such example that helps to build sustainable value through cross-enterprise leadership.

We have presented the challenges and opportunities of cross-enterprise leadership and it is important to convey that it is not for the faint of heart. Anyone who has spent any time in organizations knows the stranglehold that organization structures and reward-and-compensation systems can have on both innovation and execution. Wherever you sit in the organization chart, cross-enterprise leadership means that you must deliver on the mandate of your position, but look more broadly to opportunities that enable you and your organization to better deliver on that mandate. We have described the competencies of the cross-enterprise leader that enable this, and in doing so we have emphasized the critical component of aspiration. Yet it is clear that this aspiration must be aligned across the organization and, where possible, across organizations. One of the challenges of cross-enterprise leadership is the lack of alignment with individuals, departments, business units and organizations working at cross-purpose. If you are Sony, you would have to take a hard look at yourself to ask why Apple invented and asserted its leadership with the iPod and iTunes when you had the technology and music in your grasp years earlier. And industries have been transformed by organizations that have worked cross-enterprise to develop systems of interconnectivity—witness Wal-Mart and the associated transformation of retail. But every organization and virtually every industry has a story to tell like this.

On the one hand the challenges can be daunting, yet on the other, the fact that they are so suggests the possibility for competitive advantage and superior performance for those who can overcome them. Failing to understand the need for cross-enterprise leadership leaves organizations exposed on several fronts. There are fault lines within organizations, as revealed in organization charts that define the silos of organizations. These fault lines also exist between organizations where risk resides but often goes unnoticed because no one owns them or manages them. Scott Snook's account of the factors that led to the accidental shoot-down of the two U.S. Black Hawk helicopters in his book *Friendly Fire* is a detailed account of what these fault lines look like and how they develop. Although these risks come in the form of threats, they also present missed opportunity. Cross-enterprise leaders are better able to mitigate the risks and seize the opportunities that lie in the white spaces within organizations and between organizations.

Cross-enterprise leadership is not for the faint of heart because it requires energy and commitment even when goals are aligned. When goals are misaligned the task is even more heroic. The importance of goal alignment and aspiration is even more apparent when you consider the enormous challenge of coordination required for cross-enterprise leadership to work. The bother factor alone is enough for individuals to yearn for simpler times and circumstances. Cross-enterprise leaders know that complexity and coordination is inevitable, and they understand that part of the risk in execution is that there are many involved who do not share the same goals and aspirations.

The theme of "complacency" came up often when we spoke with leaders in our effort to learn from the economic crisis. Complacency in organizations is a reality that cross-enterprise leaders must work actively to understand and influence. The gap that cross-enterprise leadership must fill with respect to structure, reward systems, goal alignment and aspiration is compounded by associated elements of accountability and responsibility. It is inevitable that leaders will be accountable for things for which they do not have responsibility. While this has always been the case for leaders, it is compounded in the case of cross-enterprise leadership.

It is important to reiterate that cross-enterprise leadership applies broadly to all types of organizations and to individuals at all levels of the organization. Without cross-enterprise leaders throughout the organization, it will be nearly impossible for a leader at the top of the organization to lead in a cross-enterprise fashion. And while we have used the term leadership, we understand that term to embrace the notion of followership, a factor that seems to be lost on many leaders. As Ivey Professor Jane Howell notes, leadership is a relationship jointly produced by leaders and followers. With cross-enterprise leadership there is distributed leadership, and it means that at almost every turn individuals are both leading and supporting other leaders.

Cross-enterprise leadership is indeed challenging. However, it is not an option or something that is simply nice to have. Failing to lead in a cross-enterprise fashion incurs risk in the form of failing to identify and mitigate risks, and also failing to identify and take advantage of opportunities. Cross-enterprise leadership is not the panacea to all that can go wrong in organizations; however, it goes a long way in the direction of what can go right.

In the Foreword to this book, Ivey Dean Carol Stephenson asked us to "Imagine what might have happened if business and government leaders had better appreciated the interconnectedness of different organizations, markets and economies. Imagine if more leaders had focused on long-term results, not just short-term returns. Imagine if more leaders had acted with vision, honesty and integrity." She concluded that she has no doubt that the outcome would have been much different—and much better—for economies, for industries, for markets and for the customers, investors and employees who play a role in them. There is a compelling need for a new leadership approach—an approach that we call cross-enterprise leadership.

~Index~